HOW YOU GOT SCREWED

HOW YOU GOT SCREWED

WHAT BIG BANKS, BIG GOVERNMENT, AND BIG BUSINESS DON'T WHAT YOU TO KNOW—

AND WHAT YOU CAN DO ABOUT IT

ALLEN MARSHALL

Skyhorse Publishing

To Mary, the love of my life.

Skyhorse Publishing books may be purchased in bulk at special discounts for sales promotion, corporate gifts, fund-raising, or educational purposes. Special editions can also be created to specifications. For details, contact the Special Sales Department, Skyhorse Publishing, 307 West 36th Street, 11th Floor, New York, NY 10018 or info@skyhorsepublishing.com.

Skyhorse® and Skyhorse Publishing® are registered trademarks of Skyhorse Publishing, Inc.®, a Delaware corporation.

Visit our website at www.skyhorsepublishing.com.

10 9 8 7 6 5 4 3 2 1

Library of Congress Cataloging-in-Publication Data is available on file.

Cover design by Rain Saukas
Cover photo credit: iStock

ISBN: 978-1-51072-592-8
Ebook ISBN: 978-1-51072-593-5

Printed in the United States of America

CONTENTS

INTRODUCTION

I remember playing a game of Monopoly with a friend when I was maybe ten or eleven years old. I was doing well, but I was still losing—and that's when I realized that my friend, who was acting as the bank, was cheating by secretly moving money from the bank over to his own pile. Once I figured this out, I quit the game: Why play when it's impossible to win?

In a nutshell, that's what's happening to you in today's America. Throughout your entire childhood, you were told about the American Dream, and how if you worked hard and did the right things, you could build a good life for yourself. If you're reading this, then you've figured out that something went wrong: Either someone's cheating, or they changed the rules without telling you.

I'm here to tell you that this is exactly what happened. The generations before you actually did have a real shot at achieving their dreams. However, over time, so many people cheated and used shortcuts to achieving their goals, that they ended up changing the nature and accessibility of American Dream. They rigged the game, and now that it's your turn to play, they've made it almost impossible for you to win.

WHO IS THIS BOOK FOR?

Do any of the following criteria describe you?

- You're carrying huge amounts of college debt.
- You're an adult still living with your parents because you can't afford to move out.
- You're not able to find a job that pays a livable amount of money.
- You want to get married, but you can't afford it.
- Prices keep going up, but your income doesn't follow.
- You've got health insurance but can't afford medical care due to the high deductibles.
- You joined some movement like Operation Wall Street or the Tea Party, or followed a revolutionary politician like Ron Paul or Bernie Sanders, and didn't see anything change.
- You feel that something's not right, even though the government and the media keep telling you otherwise.

Then this book is for you. I've intended it to serve as a starting point: A quick, easy-to-read overview of the forces that have an impact on your life in some way, showing how they work—by design—to rob you of your rights, your money, and your potential. Although not comprehensive in scope, it should introduce you to these topics so you can get a sense of what's actually happening. You can—and should—broaden and deepen your understanding of these issues, especially the examples that pertain most to yourself. It concludes with some suggestions for what to do with this new information, but that's a starting point as well: It's up to you to decide what to do next.

WHO AM I?

Allen Marshall is an alias.

In reality, I'm a typical middle-aged guy. I've achieved my own American Dream, with a wife, two kids, two dogs, and a house with a white picket fence in the suburbs (seriously).

I've pretty much got it made—but over time, as I learned about how the game is rigged, how the odds are stacked against the next generation, I've come to realize that my kids are going to face huge hurdles in achieving their dreams—hurdles I didn't have to face. And it's not just my kids: I realized that a lot of people in my generation, and the majority of people younger than me, are in the same boat.

Not only are most of them destined for a life of frustration and unfulfilled dreams, but the system that's holding them down is the same system that's choking the life out of this country. And it's all because some of the people who came before us decided to rewrite the rules of the game to benefit themselves and hurt the rest of us.

WHY WRITE THIS BOOK?

I struggle every day with what to do about the challenges that I see so many people facing. My kids are too young for me to share all this with them; they're not ready. But there are lots of people who are, and just need a little assistance in seeing the big picture.

That's why I wrote this book. If you read it and see things in a different way—if it helps you understand how the system is rigged against you—then you'll have the chance to do something about it.

I can't tell you what that "something" is. I don't think these problems can be solved with marches and protests; I don't even really think they can be solved through voting, unless we actually start voting for people who tell the truth and tell us up front about the hard choices we have to make. Perhaps we all just have to pull out of the system entirely. That's for you and your peers to decide.

I'm just trying to do my part by sharing information, along with my wishes and prayers that others can pick up the torch and carry it forward.

A WORD ABOUT DATA

Throughout this book, you'll notice that I raise concerns about some institution, and then later quote that same institution's research or data. For example, I talk about the Federal Reserve working contrary to the interests of our country, yet continue to reference information from the Federal Reserve Economic Data (FRED) system from the Federal Reserve Bank of St. Louis. Or I'll talk about the flaws in the way our government calculates GDP, and then use GDP numbers as a way to track economic growth.

This is, unfortunately, unavoidable. In many cases these institutions are the only sources of information available on certain issues, or at least the only commonly-acknowledged sources. And to understand the issues covered in this book, we have got to be able to incorporate data into the discussion. However, to limit the potential for biased analysis, I follow three rules when using data:

- **Cui bono?** I try to ask myself who benefits from the data being reported and look for conflicts of interest. If the government wants to look good by reducing unemployment rates, then they have a vested interest in making those numbers look better than they actually

are. I would much rather look for an independent organization or watchdog group to provide data.

- **Look for "minimally processed" data.** I tend to rely
  on data from FRED because it is not filtered or mas-
  saged: They report on national debt levels, for example, without trying to tell me whether they're good or
  bad. In contrast, numbers like the unemployment
  rate or GDP are heavily doctored in the ways in which
  they are defined, collected, and reported, so I don't
  consider those reliable at all.
- **Compare similar numbers.** In cases where the risk of
  corrupted data is high (such as unemployment rates
  or GDP), I try to use them more for comparisons
  rather than for an objective picture. For example, if
  every country has similarly flawed ways of measuring
  GDP, we can use those numbers to gauge the relative
  sizes of those countries' economies regardless of the
  accuracy of the information. If we look at unemployment rates over time, we can get a sense of trends,
  even if the specific values are wrong.

You'll see the Latin words "caveat emptor" a lot in this book; they
mean "buyer beware," which is a mindset too many people have
lost. When it comes to data, it means you shouldn't automatically
accept what you're being told, whether it comes from a watchdog
group or the Federal Reserve. I keep a skeptical eye and look for
multiple sources to come together in a complete picture, and I
would encourage you to be similarly skeptical. Collect information to prove to yourself that something is true, and don't rely
wholly on anyone—including me—to tell you.

CONTACTING THE AUTHOR

Poet Don Marquis reportedly said, "Publishing a volume of verse is like dropping a rose petal down the Grand Canyon and waiting for the echo." Writing a book like this one results in a similar lack of feedback, and I'd be very interested in hearing your thoughts. If you'd like to share your reactions to what's written here, tell me what you think I got wrong, share related information with me, or ask questions, you can email me directly at Allen@DefiantLiving.com. I promise to respond to you as quickly as I'm able.

PART I

THE MONEY MASTERS

1

How you're getting screwed by . . .
THE MONEY SYSTEM

The few who understand the system, will either be so interested from its profits or so dependent on its favors, that there
will be no opposition from that class . . . Let me issue and control a nation's money and I care not who writes the laws.

—Mayer Amschel Rothschild (1744–1812),
founder of the House of Rothschild.

THE POINT:

Our entire money system is based on debt, which requires constant
expansion (in other words, inflation and even more debt). This means
that your money keeps losing value, and they're going to keep pushing you—and everyone else—to take on as much debt as you can.
It's theft, and it's debt slavery.

There's an old saying that "a fish doesn't know it's in water."
Meaning that when something surrounds us so completely, is
such an elemental part of our lives, it's easy for that thing to be
invisible. Our money system is like that.

We take money for granted—it just "is." Nobody thinks about
it, or questions it. We know what dollars and cents are, and we

know that we can trade them for things we want, and we know that they're a store of value. Right?

The truth is, our money system has not been around forever—it's a fairly recent invention—and it was designed to steal value from you.

1913: THE FED COMES ON THE SCENE

The U.S. Constitution says that Congress is supposed to manage our money system—specifically, "To coin Money, regulate the Value thereof . . . ".[1] But in 1913, Congress punted, and gave up that authority by privatizing the endeavor to an entity called the Federal Reserve. The government does have some input into this central bank, since it appoints the bank's governors. However, the twelve regional banks that make up the Federal Reserve are all privately owned, with banks being the only stockholders![2]

Why is this a big deal? Because a private organization owned by banks—not a public institution—now runs our money supply. And because they're banks, and banks make their money by lending money, they naturally designed a debt-based system. That means the money system has to grow constantly, which means your dollars are worth less every year. It's a system that works for them, not for you.

FROM A GOLD STANDARD TO NO STANDARD

Originally, the Fed was held somewhat in check by the nation's gold standard, which means that money can be exchanged for physical gold at any time at a set price. This prevents a country from printing money or otherwise devaluing the currency: If people sense that the currency has less value, they'll exchange it for the physical gold, and eventually the Federal Reserve would run out. This system worked for quite a while, with an ounce of gold equal to $20.67 for nearly a century until 1933, when President Franklin Roosevelt attempted to confiscate peoples' physical gold while raising the exchange rate to $35 per ounce.[3] This allowed him to introduce a one-time devaluation of the currency, part of his strategy to counter the deflation during the Great Depression.

Unfortunately, the desire to print money—to increase what the government could spend—was too great, and in 1971 Richard Nixon took the country off the gold standard, to a pure fiat system. By cutting the constraints on government spending that a gold standard imposed, he was able to "have his cake and eat it too," continuing to spend heavily on the Vietnam War without having to rein in the expanding welfare state at home.

What's a fiat system? The word "Fiat" is Latin, and translates as "let it be done." It's a government dictate saying that this is money because we say it is, even though it's not backed by anything real. Which is a stunning thought: The only reason the money in your pocket has any value is because we all believe that it does, nothing more. And that collective faith—that this piece of paper has some kind of inherent value—allows them to play all kinds of games behind the scenes.

THE 2 PERCENT TARGET

By deciding that money isn't backed by anything but faith, the government and the Fed were able to dramatically increase the amount of money in circulation. Since it wasn't backed by anything, there was nothing to stop them from expanding the money supply as they saw fit.

What happens when you have roughly the same number of products and services, but drop more and more money into the system? At first, it works great: You're able to buy more things before people catch on. But eventually the system adjusts, and prices go up to balance the system. You can see what happened to prices since the Fed was founded in the following chart:[4]

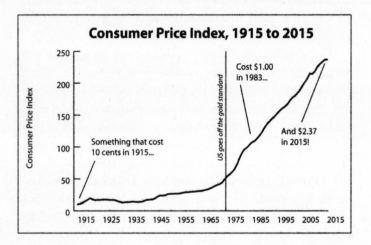

Consumer Price Index, 1915 to 2015

Something that cost 10 cents in 1915...

US goes off the gold standard

Cost $1.00 in 1983...

And $2.37 in 2015!

Believe it or not, this price inflation is official Fed policy: Even though they have a clear mandate to make sure prices remain *stable* (written into law in 1977), they interpret this as making sure prices *increase at a stable rate*, a target of 2 percent per year, which is an awfully deceptive interpretation of their mandate.

Do you know what 2 percent inflation does to you?

- In 1 year, something that cost you $1.00 today will cost you $1.02. Your dollar will lose 2 percent of its value.
- In 10 years, something that cost you $1.00 today will

cost you $1.22. Your dollar will lose 18 percent of its value.

- In 20 years, something that cost you $1.00 today will cost you $1.49. Your dollar will lose 33 percent of its value.

- In 50 years, something that cost you $1.00 today will cost you $2.69. Your dollar will lose 63 percent of its value.

They're stealing value from you on purpose. Because they know most people don't know or understand what they're doing, and because it's a very gradual process.

Of course, they have a good cover story as to why they push for inflation: They say that since growing economies produce inflation, then logically, producing inflation will result in growing economies. As David Collum sarcastically notes in his 2016 year-end review, "That's like warming a corpse to 98.6 degrees (maybe even a few tenths warmer) to bring it to life. Hey guys: try jolting it with electricity while rubbing your palms together and cackling. I'm sure it will work."[5]

DEBT . . . LOTS AND LOTS OF DEBT

There's an important piece missing here: How does all of this money get added to the economy without people realizing what's happening? It happens through the creation of debt—people, companies, and governments borrowing money.

And we have been borrowing money at an amazing rate. In fact, as you can see in the chart on the next page,[6] we've grown our total public debt (personal, business, and government combined) from $436 billion in 1950 to $63.5 trillion in 2015! We've doubled the amount of debt we collectively hold seven times since 1950; to double it again we'll have to reach $115 trillion, and that just doesn't seem possible.

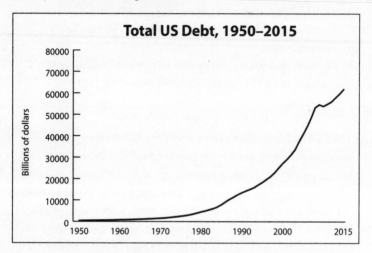

This brings up an interesting point: That debt can't grow forever. Just as trees can't grow to the sky, there's a limit on how big our debt level can get. People, businesses, and governments can only borrow as much as they can service (in other words, their ability to make the payments).

So if borrowing capacity is limited, how can the Fed—which requires ever-growing debt—keep the game going?

CENTRAL BANKERS GONE WILD

If you look at the chart above, you'll notice a slight bump in the line, when the total volume of debt dropped slightly. That minor bump was felt in a major way: It was the 2008 financial crisis, showing what happens to the economy when we can't continue to increase debt at the needed speed.

That crisis threw central bankers into a panic, and they began basically making up policies as they went along. And if that scares the hell out of you, it should: The thought of a bunch of academics with no real-world experience trying things that had never been done before, with their hands on the levers of economies around the world, is a truly terrifying thought. So what exactly have they done since 2009 to get debt growing again?

Creating an Illusion of Health

The Fed is under the impression that if they make the financial markets look better than they are, people will feel more confident and start to spend, thereby actually bringing the economy back to life. They've therefore made a real effort to fool us into believing that everything is back on track, regardless of our real-world experiences.

One example is their suspension of the "mark to market" rule. The Financial Accounting Standards Board (FASB) sets the rules for acceptable accounting practices among financial institutions, and one of their bedrock rules was that assets had to be valued at whatever the market would actually pay for them. On March 16, 2009, as the effects of the 2008 financial crisis were increasing, FASB abandoned that rule (FAS 157) in favor of a "mark to model" standard, in which banks could value assets at whatever their models—not that day's market prices—told them they were worth. This approach, often called "mark to fantasy," saved them from displaying a huge hole on their balance sheets.[7]

Another driver is the fact that the Federal Reserve was making a blatant attempt to juice the stock market, doing whatever they could to push it higher so we all felt that the economy was strong. As Richard Fisher, former president of the Dallas Federal Reserve, said on CNBC, "What the Fed did, and I was part of that group, is we front-loaded a tremendous market rally starting in 2009, March of 2009 . . . We front-loaded, at the Federal Reserve, an enormous rally in order to accomplish a wealth effect."[8] And they may still be at it: There is a widespread suspicion of a "Plunge Protection Team," possibly at the Fed or driven by the President's Working Group on Financial Markets, that actively works in the markets to prevent large drops and move the indices higher.[9]

Bad Debt: Buying It and Hiding It

And what to do about the bad debt out there—the loans that the banks made that people can't service on a regular basis? The Fed helped quite a bit with that, buying many of those nonperforming loans (especially mortgage debt after the housing crisis); it now has just under $4.5 trillion dollars on its balance sheet including just over $1.7 trillion in those mortgage-backed securities.[10]

Beyond that, banks have adopted a policy commonly known as "extend and pretend," which means that if someone can't pay their loan back, you give them an extension and pretend that the loan hasn't gone bad. This was common practice right after the 2008 crisis to handle residential and commercial real estate loans, and even as of 2013, four of the biggest banks still held $57 billion in such loans on their books.[11] More recently, when bad debts started to show up from energy companies (the fracking industry was heavily debt-financed, and dependent on much higher oil prices), analysts fully expect to see banks relying on the same strategy to hide those bad loans as well.[12]

Lowering Interest Rates

One way they can keep things going is to lower interest rates. Remember that you can only borrow to the level at which you can manage to make payments; therefore, if they lower the interest rate, you can borrow more than you could before. If you have a $1 million loan and it costs you $50,000 in payments at 5 percent interest, lowering the interest rate means your payments are lower—and you can borrow more. If they lower rates to 2.5 percent, for example, you could then borrow $2 million with that same $50,000 per year payment.

That's why interest rates keep going lower. The Fed has been holding its official rate near zero for years, and many countries, such as Japan, are actually issuing bonds at negative interest rates! While the U.S. hasn't moved into negative interest rates yet, and is currently raising rates at the time of this writing, the Fed has appeared open to the idea, and it wouldn't surprise anyone to see it happen the next time the economy stumbles.

When you hear that negative interest rates are unprecedented, understand that this absolutely true. As Matthew Borin notes:

> Central banks are treading in uncharted waters. Sidney Homer and Richard Sylla, the authors of *A History of Interest Rates*, found no instance of negative rates in 5,000 years. Now there are $11.7 trillion invested in negative-yield sovereign debt, including $7.9 trillion in Japanese government bonds and over $1 trillion in both French and German sovereign debt.
>
> [The publisher of Grant's Interest Rate Observer Jim] Grant posed a tongue-in-cheek question: "If these are the first sub-zero interest rates in 5,000 years, is this not the worst economy since 3,000 BC?"[13]

Of course, pushing interest rates down makes borrowing more attractive. But there remains the question as to whether that borrowing was used for productive purposes. Nonfinancial corporations, for example, saw their debt levels collectively increase from $6.4 trillion to $8 trillion between 2013 and 2015; during that same time, they used $1.3 trillion to buy back shares of their companies,[14] which boosted their share prices and did little else except produce big bonuses for executives through corporate stock options mechanisms.

And on the flip side, those low interest rates have been causing untold damage to retirees trying to live off their savings, and to businesses like insurance companies and pension funds that rely on the interest payments from the safest investments like bonds.

What does all this mean? It means that our government passed an important responsibility on to private companies that don't have our interests at heart, and those private companies are trying to saturate us with debt so they can steal value from our money and keep the game going as long as possible.

2

How you're getting screwed by . . .
WALL STREET

It is well enough that people of the nation do not understand our banking and money system, for if they did, I believe there would be a revolution before tomorrow morning.
—Henry Ford, founder of the Ford Motor Company.

THE POINT:

If you were looking for a single industry to represent the kind of unfair, unethical, and illegal behavior that's hurting everyday Americans, you wouldn't have to look any further than the financial industry. From extorting politicians to bail out their bad decisions to manipulating every market they can, they just pay a small percentage of their profits as a fine on those rare occasions when they get caught, and move on to the next hustle.

It's very hard to write about the ways in which big banks, investment companies, and others are taking advantage of you. The reason: The financial industry makes everything as complicated and confusing as possible so they can get away with their scams. I will try to make everything as simple as possible so people can understand it.

I'll admit it: My eyes glaze over when people start talking about my investing options. I would fall asleep if I tried to read all of the paperwork in my mortgage documents. And that's what they count on: That the more complicated they make things, the fewer ordinary citizens will be able to understand them, and that's where they have an opportunity to take advantage of us.

Let's look at the big-picture evidence.

THE FINANCIAL CRISIS

Remember the big financial crisis in 2008 and 2009? That was caused by two things working together. The first was making crazy loans to people who had no chance of paying them back. The second was making insanely complicated financial products out of those loans, and then selling those to investors without being honest about what they really were.

But when it all blew up, and all that dishonest, unethical, and illegal behavior was exposed, what happened? Did anybody get fired? Did anybody get arrested or go to jail?

No, what happened was that Congress passed a $700 billion bailout package to save the industry, and the Federal Reserve did backflips to support them as well, lowering interest rates and buying a lot of their bad loans.

SINCE 2009

After that, they just kept doing what they were doing. They weren't worried about going to jail: No one involved with all these shady deals was ever arrested, and in fact Eric Holder, Attorney General of the U.S. at the time, even came out on TV and said that the big banks were too big to prosecute.[15]

Since then, the big banks and investment firms have been on a tear, manipulating just about every financial market there is and making billions from all sorts of fraudulent activities. And if they get caught? They pay a fine—a small percentage of their profits from these activities—and go on to the next scam.

A nonprofit called Good Jobs First tracks these kinds of violations, and had this to say:[16]

> Since the beginning of 2010 major U.S. and foreign-based banks have paid more than $160 billion in penalties (fines and settlements) to resolve cases brought against them by the Justice Department and federal regulatory agencies. Bank of America alone accounts for $56 billion of the total and JPMorgan Chase another $28 billion. Fourteen banks have each accumulated penalty amounts in excess of $1 billion, and five of those are in excess of $10 billion.

They list the following types of violations and fines since 2010 on the part of the banks:

Type of Case	Penalties
Toxic securities and mortgage abuses	$118,351,845,751
Violations of rules prohibiting business with enemy countries	$15,281,854,381
Manipulation of foreign exchange markets	$7,386,000,000
Manipulation of interest rate benchmarks	$5,473,000,000
Assisting tax evasion	$2,353,633,153
Credit card abuses	$2,168,800,000
Failing to report suspicious behavior by Bernard Madoff	$2,161,000,000
Inadequate money-laundering controls	$1,265,000,000
Discriminatory practices	$939,300,000
Manipulation of energy markets	$897,900,000
Other major cases	$3,771,900,000
TOTAL	**$160,050,233,285**

This list doesn't do justice to how extreme some of these crimes are. Fines for "inadequate money-laundering controls," for example, include cases such as HSBC laundering money for "Saudi Arabian terrorists, Mexican drug cartels and rogue regimes in North Korea and Cuba"[17] and Wachovia laundering billions of dollars for Mexican cocaine smugglers.[18]

And again—no one goes to jail for any of this, they just pay back a small portion of the profits and move on to the next shady deal.

So why should you care? Well, aside from the obvious double standard of justice (I bet if you did any of these things you'd be prosecuted pretty quickly), you're paying for all of this. That $700 billion bailout from Congress? That was tax money—your money. Those fines? That comes out of your pocket too, in the form of higher fees and lower returns on your savings and investments.

And a final point: if banks start failing again, it will be depositors—not taxpayers—on the hook for the losses this time. If you think you'll get your money back when your bank fails, think again: The FDIC, which guarantees your bank account, only has around $67 billion in reserves (cash and Treasuries)[19] compared with the $11.4 trillion on deposit in commercial banks.[20] Even though not all of that $11.4 trillion is covered by the FDIC (they only guarantee up to $250,000 per account), there's still no chance they'll be able to cover the majority of losses that depositors face if things go south.

WHAT ABOUT INVESTING?

Okay, so you can't trust the banking system. What about the stock market and your other investments? Banks aside, are the financial markets safe and fair?

Manipulation

You see the word "manipulation" in several of the fine categories above? In fact, banks and financial services companies have been manipulating most financial markets for the past several years in order to make bigger profits for themselves and their friends, and less for you.

They have acknowledged or been convicted of manipulating the following markets:[21]

- Gold and silver markets
- Other commodities, including uranium mining, petroleum products, aluminum, ownership and operation of airports, toll roads, ports, and electricity
- Oil prices
- Mortgage markets
- The Treasury market
- Currency markets
- Derivatives
- Energy prices
- Interest rates, including LIBOR (which sets many other rates)

And, as noted above, none of these crimes results in jail time for any of the financiers involved: They simply pay a small fine, considered the cost of doing business, and move on to the next thing.

Actually, that's admittedly not entirely true: From time to time, someone is arrested and prosecuted for market manipulation. The catch is that they have to be a "small fish," not employed by an important financial institution and not politically connected.

Consider the case of Navinder Singh Sarao, a thirty-six year old Indian working out of a modest suburban home in Hounslow, near London. A successful trader, he was engaged in spoofing the markets in 2010 (an illegal practice in which you make a large bid, withdraw it as others react to your bid, and then trade based on their reaction). Authorities argue that he caused the 2010 "Flash Crash" in U.S. markets, though experts doubt that he was the primary cause.[22] He was extradited to the U.S., recently pled guilty to all charges, and is expected to serve a sentence somewhere between six and thirty years.[23]

If this was a trader with one of the major banks, and not a reclusive day trader who lived with his parents and didn't know how to drive a car, do you think he would be sitting in jail today? Or would his connected firm have paid a fine and moved forward with no other repercussions?

Derivatives

Speaking of things going south: Nothing has more potential to blow up the financial system than the derivatives market, a problem that was not only not resolved after the 2008 crisis, but has gotten dramatically larger.

Derivatives are one of those extremely complicated products that financial wizards love, but that few of the rest of us understand (which may be part of the reason they love them). There are many different types, but you can consider them to be insurance on other financial products or events. Unlike regular insurance markets, however, the derivative market is unregulated, and the industry has done everything in its power to keep it that way.

If you've issued a bunch of loans and you're worried about people not paying, you could buy a derivative that pays off if they don't pay. If you're a farmer and you're worried what the price of corn will be when it's time to sell, you can buy a derivative to protect yourself. That's pretty reasonable in theory.

CASE STUDY: WELLS FARGO

Suppose that a friend of yours asked you to hold his wallet for a few minutes—and while he was gone you rifled through it, copied down his Social Security number, and later used it to apply for a credit card in his name. According to the U.S. Department of Justice, that's a felony called identity theft, and if convicted, you'd be facing up to fifteen years in jail and on the hook for fines and for paying back all that you stole.[30]

Now suppose that you made hundreds, or even thousands, of your friends do the same thing to all of their friends. What do you think your punishment would be? Well, if your name was "Wells Fargo," you'd find that it wasn't much of a punishment at all.

Like most businesses, Wells Fargo sets sales goals for the people who work with their customers. In Wells Fargo's case, this involved encouraging current customers to increase the number of services they use from the bank. If you had a checking account, they'd ask you to also open a savings account, take out a credit card, apply for a car loan, and so on. As the *New York Times* notes, "The bank's chief executive, John Stumpf, has often stated his goal that each Wells customer should have at least eight accounts with the company. That aggressive target has made the bank's stock a darling on Wall Street . . . "[31]

There's just one problem: people don't want that many accounts with the bank. So if you're an employee at Wells Fargo, responsible for boosting the number of products per customer and being threatened with termination if you don't, what do you do?

Apparently, what you do is open up new accounts in your customer's name without telling them, using approaches such as the following (according to a complaint filed by the Los Angeles City Attorney):[32]

In the practice known at Wells Fargo as "pinning," a Wells Fargo banker obtains a debit card number, and personally sets the PIN, often to 0000, without customer authorization. "Pinning" permits a banker to enroll a customer in online banking, for which the banker would receive a solution (sales credit). To bypass computer prompts requiring customer contact information, bankers impersonate the customer online, and input false generic email addresses such as 1234@wellsfargo.com, noname@wellsfargo.com, or none@wellsfargo.com to ensure that the transaction is completed, and that the customer remains unaware of the unauthorized activity.

What's amazing is the scope of this fraud: It appears to have started way back in 2005 and ended just recently, and resulted in the opening of around two million customer accounts and credit cards without authorization.[33] And not only were 5,300 employees fired when caught doing this, but many whistleblowers claim that they were similarly fired for trying to report that it was happening through internal channels.[34]

Did anyone go to jail? Of course not. The CEO blamed the employees, not the company culture,[35] and the bank paid a fine of $185 million. Stumpf and the head of retail banking, Carrie Tolstedt, retired, giving up $60 million in stock in light of the scandal, but at the same time taking home $350 million in golden parachute compensation.[36]

If there's any justice here, it's that the public actually took notice and punished the company as consumers, with the number of new accounts being opened dropping by a substantial 44 percent.[37] But that may be the only justice, as banks get away with things that you and I would go to jail for, and employees get punished for actions while executives walk out with hundreds of millions of dollars.

3

How you're getting screwed by . . .
THE HOUSING MARKET

Ask most people who live in a home and have a mortgage on it whether they own their own home and the answer is almost guaranteed to be a resounding "yes." Yet it's the wrong answer. Technically speaking, until they have paid the mortgage off, they don't own it. Herein lies the difference between reality and illusion, between ownership and control. This confusion lies not only at the individual level, but also at the heart of government thinking.

—Dambisa Moyo, *How the West Was Lost*[38]

THE POINT:

There's a lot of hype about the value of owning a home—you've been told that it's part of the American Dream, and a bedrock component of your financial security. But a hard look at the reality of the housing market reveals tremendous risk for buyers in an era when supply is about to outstrip demand, and those in the market face various other headwinds.

"A home is an investment," the real estate agents tell you—but it's their job to tell you that, and to sell you on the biggest, most expensive house possible. The truth is, while owning a home may produce financial rewards in a limited set of circumstances, in most cases the only people benefiting financially from your home purchase are the real estate agent and the banker writing the mortgage.

If you choose to look at your home as an investment, understand that it's an expensive one that requires ongoing infusions of time and money, and that you'll only see a return if market conditions are better than when you yourself bought the home. And whether you see it as an investment or not, understand that the financial industry has utterly ruined housing in the pursuit of every possible dollar.

ARE HOMES AN INVESTMENT?

The value of a home, like any asset, is based on supply and demand. Specifically, how many homes are available, and how many people want—and are able to afford—a home.

Throughout America's boom years, demand was much higher than supply: The population was growing, families were expanding, incomes were growing, and the standard of living was increasing, meaning that people were not only looking for homes, they were looking for bigger and better homes. Home prices went up and went up quickly, thanks to this demand and also thanks to the increase in financing made possible by the bankers (more on this later in the chapter).

So yes, at a certain point in time, you could consider your home to be an investment: All of the market forces were going your way, and you could reasonably expect to sell your home for more—perhaps much more—than you paid for it.

But market conditions change, and the tailwinds that boosted home prices are turning into headwinds that will fundamentally change the idea of a home as an investment.

Demographics

Baby Boomers, those born between 1946 and 1964, are the largest single population group in America, and they have an outsized influence on the U.S. housing market: In 2013, the Federal Reserve estimated that households led by people age fifty-five and older controlled two-thirds of all home equity, while one federal estimate puts the aggregate value of their houses at close to $8 trillion.[39]

When it comes to demand for "more" and "better" homes over the past forty years, Boomers have been the ones driving that trend. The average home size increased by more than 1,000 square feet between 1973 and 2013, from an average 1,660 to 2,679 square feet; and given smaller households, that has resulted in a near-doubling of living space per person.[40]

As this population nears retirement age (the first Boomer turned 65 in 2011), they're breaking with tradition: Many are continuing to work, and as a fitter, mentally younger generation, they're in no rush to sell the family home and downsize. That means they're staying put longer than their parents did, resulting in a tightening of the housing market (i.e., fewer listings), and this reduced supply is keeping the number of listings lower and prices higher.[41]

However, as Fannie Mae researchers note, "Boomers will not inhabit this vast inventory of single-family homes forever. When large numbers of Boomers eventually begin to vacate their single-family homes, their actions will reverberate through the housing market and will likely lead to a substantial increase in the demand for other shelter types, including apartments."[42]

Which leads to the question: Who will buy all those large, expensive, single-family homes?

Ability to Pay

The generations coming up behind the Boomers—and the ones we would expect to buy the Boomers' homes—are Generation X (1965–1984) and, with a slight overlap, the Millennials (1982–2004).[43] Are either in a position to absorb the inventory left behind when the Boomers finally move on to smaller homes, apartments, and retirement communities?

Don't look to Generation X to pick up the slack. This generation is smaller than the one before it or after it—65.7 million people, versus 74.9 million Boomers and 75.3 million Millennials, in 2015.[44] They are also the generation with the highest levels of debt: The average forty-four year old Gen-Xer had household debt of $142,077, versus the average Boomer when he or she was forty-four years old, who had just $88,553 in household debt (inflation adjusted).[45] What's more, Generation X adults carry about the same amount in student loans—$20,000—as people fresh out of college do, and struggle to prepare for the costs to send their own children to college.[46] This group doesn't have the size or financial means to snap up all those soon-to-be-sold Boomer houses.

As for the Millennials, who are currently (2017) between 13 and 35 years old, they have around the same number of people as the Boomers, but at least for those who are adults, their attitudes and financial resources are markedly different. Young adults ages 18 to 34 are more likely to live with a parent than in any other arrangement, with 32.1 percent doing so; this even exceeds those married or living together in their own household (31.6 percent), a record low.[47] And while 80 percent of Millennials see owning a home as part of the American dream, there are a number of factors preventing them from doing so, including the high cost of rent, access to credit, availability of affordable homes, existing debt (especially college debt), and inability to make payments.[48]

Interest Rates

While people generally talk in terms of a house's list price, the actual decision usually comes down to the monthly payment, with most financial experts suggesting a monthly payment of no more than 25–30 percent of income. One of the biggest factors in the monthly payment is the interest rate on your mortgage: At 4 percent interest, a $200,000 loan (30-year mortgage) would require monthly payments of $1,343; at 8 percent, it would result in monthly payments of $1,856.

One of the tailwinds over the past thirty-five years is that interest rates have been dropping, with thirty-year mortgage rates peaking at 18.4 percent in 1981, and sliding all the way down to 3.5 percent in 2016.[49] The difference in payments between the two, by the way, assuming that same $200,000 loan,

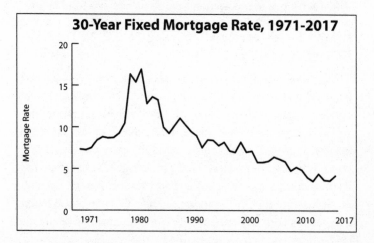

is $3,080 per month versus $898 per month. You can buy a lot
more house at the lower rate.

The fact that interest rates have effectively bottomed out and
are back on the rise (the Fed has already raised the federal funds
rate a few times in the past two years), means that mortgage payments are about to get more expensive, pushing the price of
homes back down based on the resulting monthly payments that
people are able to afford.

Homeownership Rates

Despite all the favorable tailwinds that have been with us to date,
the homeownership rate fell to a five-decade low of 62.9 percent,
a number last seen in 1965 when they started to collect this data.
There are many reasons for this, first among them the number of
homes lost after the 2006 housing bubble popped (homeownership rates were at 69 percent at that point). Going forward, I
would expect that number to continue to drop given that the tailwinds described in this section have all turned into headwinds.

HOW THE FINANCIAL INDUSTRY RUINED THE HOUSING MARKET

Back in the "good old days," mortgages were difficult to get and
required that borrowers meet strict conditions, including that
borrowers make a 20 percent minimum down payment, take out
a loan for no more than triple household income, purchase
insurance on the loan, and go through interviews and background checks. Today, however, the modern banking system has
thrown caution to the wind, and has not only come up with
exotic loan products with minimal standards, but has also found
a way to make money over and over on the loans they've already
made.

What Led to the 2008 Housing Crisis?

As noted previously, interest rates have been falling since 1981; and, after the recession that followed the dot-com stock crash in 2001, the Federal Reserve pushed down short-term rates quickly to help the economy recover.[50] This by itself was enough for us to see strong activity in the housing market after 2001.

But lower rates weren't enough to create a housing bubble; we needed some help. And that's where the banks came in.

With low rates and federal backing for loans, as well as deregulation that allowed bank mergers and more and more exotic types of lending, banks and other financial services companies opened up the floodgates on loans, lending money to anyone with a pulse. They did so on the expectation that "home prices always go up" and that even people with little income would be able to sell at a profit to cover the loans if they ran into trouble.

To build lending volume as much as possible, banks came out with some truly bizarre loan models:

- **Limited-Doc Loans**—also called "liar loans," where you provided limited verifiable information
- **No-Doc Loans**—with these loans you provided nothing more than a credit score—no proof of income, assets, or employment
- **NINJA Loans**—Loans given out to people with No Income, No Job, and no Assets, with the assumption that the price of the home would increase, making creditworthiness irrelevant
- **"Pick-a-Pay"**—Loans in which you chose how much to pay each month—either the full payment, partial payments, or even only the interest

Many of these loans offered extremely favorable terms for a limited period, such as minimal payments for three years, which allowed borrowers to buy a house at little cost and sell it at a profit before the stricter terms came about.

This fed into a housing bubble frenzy, where people began buying homes purely to flip them at higher prices, and those who decided to stay put began pulling out money through Home Equity Lines of Credit (HELOCs) to pay off bills, travel, buy cars, and of course invest in other homes. And it caused the price of houses to rocket up, from an average $207,800 in 2001 to $322,700 in 2007,[51] with some hot markets seeing much steeper increases: Las Vegas, for example, saw the median price of existing homes skyrocket from $134,500 in the year 2000 to $285,000 in 2006.[52]

And, while this was all happening out in the open, Wall Street was just as busy behind the scenes, repackaging these loans into new financial instruments and reselling them. Financial firms created asset-backed securities called Collateralized Debt

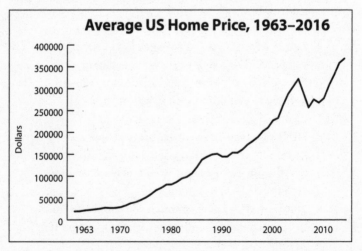

Obligations, or CDOs, which were basically large groups of mortgages grouped into different risk levels. Problems arose when firms lied about the contents of the products, with high-risk loans included in low-risk products, and when firms began to place secret derivatives bets against the products they were selling to investors. Goldman Sachs, Deutsche Bank, and Morgan Stanley were noted in particular for this strategy.[53, 54]

When the bubble popped, it caused an earthquake in the housing and financial markets. Home prices fell 20 percent nationally over the course of a couple of years, with hot markets seeing a much steeper decline. Many who had taken out risky loans simply walked away, sending the keys back to the bank; others, who had pulled out money from their home equity lines, were left deeply underwater on their homes, and many were foreclosed upon. Banks and their customers saw tremendous losses, and many mortgage firms closed.[55]

Since that time, banks have paid around $110 billion in penalties for their role in the rise and fall of the housing bubble[56]—but of course, no one was ever prosecuted or served actual jail time. And since then, we've seen a new bubble form: While there has been little of the hype that accompanied the 2001–2007 bubble, prices have risen from a post-bubble low of $257,000 in 2009 to a record $360,900 in 2016, 10 percent higher than the 2006 peak.

CNBC summarizes the argument of a new housing bubble as follows: "Housing is far less affordable today than it was back then, and the home price gains are driven not by healthy, end-user demand but by a lack of construction, artificially low interest rates, and institutional and foreign all-cash buyers."[57] Regardless of the causes, record high home prices in a market with rising interest rates, retiring and soon-to-be-downsizing Boomers, and stagnant household incomes is practically guaranteed to end badly.

4

How you're getting screwed by . . .
RETIREMENT PROMISES

Remember, this is important: Never trust that you will be saved by anyone.

—Amanda Boyden, *Pretty Little Dirty*

THE POINT:

Most people have an expectation that they'll be taken care of later in life thanks to government programs like Social Security and Medicare, private or public pensions, or through their own efforts to build up their net worth. In reality, it was never possible for governments and corporations to fulfill the promises they made to you, and those assets you saved may not be worth what you think they will be, when it's time to cash them in.

There is a predictable pattern to life: We start out as dependent children; grow to be independent adults; and, inevitably, become dependent again as we move into old age. We know this is coming; not a single person in history has avoided it. So it's important for us to plan for that while we're in our prime.

Unfortunately, the vast majority of Americans are completely unprepared for the 100 percent certainty of old age. There are many reasons for this:

- Because we live in a debt- and credit-driven society, we have come to think only of our immediate needs and wants. There's no need to save for the things we want to buy: We just borrow the money and promise to pay for them later. This mindset not only means that we're hard-wired against saving, it also means we're probably going to grow old with a pile of debt—all those things we said we'd pay back in the future. We have some assets—notably our home equity—but all that debt keeps our net worth low.

- We're about to deal with a huge demographic bubble—the aging of the huge Baby Boomer population—which will result in a selling frenzy of the assets they accumulated in better times. Asset prices will crash due to little demand and huge supply of those assets.

- The government has promised to take care of us in our old age thanks to programs like Social Security and Medicare, while many big businesses, along with the government, have similarly promised to take care of their employees through pensions. These promises—which are actually false promises, in that they cannot be met—have allowed us to forgo our own efforts to prepare for the future.

In short, even though we know for a fact that we each need to prepare for our old age, we've been taught not to worry about it and robbed of the ability to do it. It's guaranteed that this will not end well for the majority of people in this country.

ARE AMERICANS READY TO RETIRE?

Americans are awash in debt, with credit cards, mortgages, and auto loans among the primary contributors. According to Nerd-Wallet, with additional color added by Fool.com, 69 percent of U.S. households have one or more kinds of debt, and the average level of debt carried in those households was $130,922 at the end of 2015.[58] Levels of household debt in the U.S., along with the numbers and percentages of households that carry that kind of debt, are as follows:

Type of debt	Average for households with this type of debt	Total U.S. debt of this type	Households with this type of debt	Percent of American households with this type of debt (approximate)	Overall average household debt
Credit cards	$15,762	$733 billion	46.5 million	35 percent	$5,517
Mortgages	$168,614	$8.25 trillion	48.9 million	36 percent	$60,700
Auto loans	$27,141	$1.06 trillion	39.1 million	29 percent	$7,871
Student loans	$48,172	$1.23 trillion	25.5 million	19 percent	$9,153
All debt	$130,922	$12.12 trillion	92.6 million	69 percent	$90,336

"Surely," you must think, "those numbers aren't the same for people across age groups. Young people must take on a lot of debt, while people near retirement have paid theirs off." While that's true to an extent, a lot of people enter retirement age with a lot of debt. In fact, according to the U.S. Census, in the year 2011, 60.4 percent of people in the age 65–69 bracket carried debt, and the average amount of that debt was $109,973.[59] And the debt levels of people nearing retirement age have grown over the past several years: According to data from the New York Fed, the average debt levels of people ages 55–64 have grown an average of 66 percent between 2003 and 2015.[60]

And what about the other side of the coin—savings? Those debt levels wouldn't be bad if savings were much higher. However, according to the U.S. Census, in 2011 only 21 percent of households entering retirement age (55–64) had a net worth (in other words, after debt is subtracted out) of $500,000 or more, while 43 percent have less than $100,000 in assets.[61] And for most, more than half of their net worth comes from the equity in their homes,[62] meaning they would need to sell their houses in order to live off those funds. In fact, as The Fool website reports, "According to the U.S. Census Bureau's data, the typical American's net worth at age 65 is $194,226. However, removing the benefit from home equity results in that figure plummeting to just $43,921."[63]

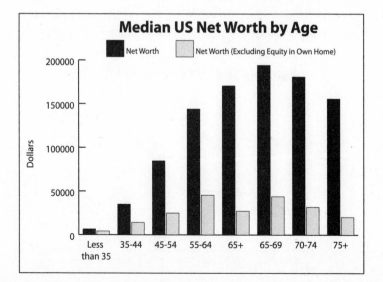

THE DEMOGRAPHIC BUBBLE

From post-war 1946 to 1964, the United States produced an epic wave of children. This generation, known as the Baby Boomers, remains the single largest generational group in the country, and as they moved through their lives from birth to seniorhood, they have had a profound impact on American society.

But their greatest impact may still be to come: The first of those Baby Boomers began to hit retirement age in 2011, and as a result the number of retirees in this country is projected to go from 40.3 million in 2010 to 82.3 million in 2040. In terms of percentages, thanks to the Boomers, retirees will go from 13 percent of the population to 21.7 percent during that time.[64]

This is a huge population shift in a very short amount of time, and it's going to hit our country like an earthquake. That's 42 million additional people drawing Social Security. Forty-two million receiving Medicare. Forty-two million needing all kinds of specialized products and services, such as elder care facilities and transportation services. And most important, 42 million

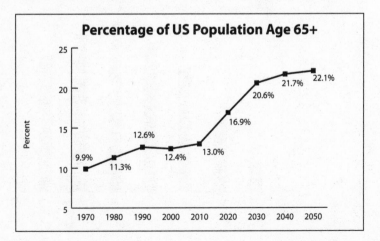

who are no longer contributing to the tax base, but instead beginning to draw from it. We'll explore some of the implications in the next few sections.

PERSONAL ASSETS

Let's consider the market theory of supply and demand:

- Suppose you go to a farmer's market and see a handful of vendors selling bananas, and hundreds of people lining up to buy them. What do you think will happen to the price of bananas?
- Suppose you go to a farmer's market and see hundreds of vendors selling bananas, and only a handful of people interested in buying them. What do you think will happen to the price of bananas?

Now substitute bananas for stocks, bonds, or homes, and think about what happens when the millions of Baby Boomers need to sell their assets into a market of people who are barely making ends meet. What's going to happen to prices for stocks, bonds, or homes?

In truth, it's not clear how much of an impact this will have on the stock market: While Boomers own 47 percent of equities, most of those are concentrated in the hands of the wealthiest 10 percent and will not be sold for living expenses.[65] But it will certainly provide a headwind, particularly as Central Banks put so much effort on boosting the prices of assets in order to create a "wealth effect" and assure people that all is well.

The greatest danger lies in the housing market. If Boomers have not saved enough to survive in retirement, and their homes represent 77 percent of their net wealth, simple logic tells us that those homes will have to be sold in order to cover their expenses (at least for a few more years). And the generations coming up behind them, including Generation X and the Millennials, have less wealth,[66] making it that much more difficult to absorb that housing surplus. The future is not bright for those who hope to sell assets at current price levels.

SOCIAL SECURITY

Many people look at Social Security as their retirement plan, and as a guaranteed right. The government does not. In the landmark *Flemming vs. Nestor* case of 1960, the Supreme Court ruled that paying into the system does not mean you have the right to receive benefits. As the Social Security Administration itself admits, "In its ruling, the Court rejected this argument [that people who pay into the system are guaranteed to receive benefits] and established the principle that entitlement to Social Security benefits is not contractual right."

The Act itself states that Congress has the authority to alter, amend, or repeal any element or rule that they want. They can raise the age for eligibility to eighty, they can limit the program to people living below the poverty line, and they can cut benefits in half if they so choose. As the Cato Institute notes, "Social Security is not an insurance program at all. It is simply a payroll tax on one side and a welfare program on the other. Your Social Security benefits are always subject to the whim of 535 politicians in Washington."[67]

At its core, Social Security is a Ponzi scheme, designed so that a large group of people would pay into a system that provided benefits for a few. It worked at the time it was designed, but the variables have changed over the years to turn it into a disaster in the making. Dr. Ken Dychtwald provides the following analysis:[68]

The problem is that current government entitlements and pensions were masterfully designed in an era when there were dozens of workers supporting each recipient, people died relatively young, most workers were diligent savers, and the government and employers were widely trusted. We now live in an era, where there are very few workers to support each retiree, most people die very old, savings rates have plummeted, and the government as well as employers' promises are not generally trusted. The ratio of 40 productive workers to each retiree that existed when Social Security was launched, has steadily shrunk, from 16 to 1 in 1950 to only 3.3 to 1 today. By 2040, it is projected that there will only be 2 workers, and perhaps as few as 1.6, to support each boomer retiree, who could be living as many as 20 to 40 years in retirement. And, between 2010 and 2030, the size of the 65+ population will grow by more than 75 percent, while the population paying payroll taxes will rise less than 5 percent.

Perhaps the most confusing and controversial element of the Social Security story is its "trust fund." The Social Security Administration will tell you that they have a trust fund of $2.8 trillion, and that those reserves will cover the system through 2034.[69] What they don't like to tell you is that those reserves aren't actually sitting around in a bank, in actual cash form: The government spent that money as soon as it came in and left an IOU in its place in the form of "special issue securities."[70] These securities are special in the sense that they cannot be sold on the open market: They can only be redeemed by the U.S. government, and since we're already running a large deficit from year to year, they'll have to raise new money to redeem those bonds, either by further increasing the deficit (i.e., even more Treasury bonds), raising taxes, or reducing spending elsewhere.

If you're still comforted by the illusion of a $2.8 trillion trust fund, it may be worth considering what happened when the government bumped up against its debt limit in 2011. When asked what would happen to Social Security checks if the government failed to raise the debt limit, President Obama said, "I cannot guarantee that those checks [he included veterans and the disabled, in addition to Social Security] go out on August 3rd if we haven't resolved this issue. Because there may simply not be the money in the coffers to do it," a statement later confirmed by Treasury Secretary Tim Geithner[71] With nearly $3 trillion in reserves, wouldn't the Social Security Administration just redeem some of those securities to ensure that payments were made? Or does this make it clear that these reserves are a convenient fiction?

Considering that 36 percent of current workers expect Social Security to be a major source of income when they retire—10 percentage points more than a decade ago[72]—it's critically important that people realize just how unreliable this program may be in the future, and what the implications of that would be both personally and to the country as a whole.

MEDICARE

Building on the foundation of social welfare established by Social Security in 1935, President Lyndon B. Johnson signed the bill that led to the establishment of Medicare (for those 65 and older, regardless of financial status) and Medicaid (for low-income citizens) in 1965. Now, just over fifty years later, Medicare serves around fifty-five million seniors and people with disabilities, and accounted for 15 percent of federal spending, $632 billion, in 2015. The program is currently funded through general funds (40 percent), payroll taxes (38 percent), and other sources.[73]

Simply put, Medicare is a bomb with a fast-burning fuse. We have a rapidly-growing population of seniors (see the information on demographics above) about to enter a system that has seen regular increases in spending: According to the Kaiser Family Foundation, Medicare spending increased at an annual average rate of 9 percent from 2000 to 2010, and then at 4.4 percent from 2010–2015.[74] Going forward, the Foundation expects average annual growth in total Medicare spending to be 7.1 percent between 2015 and 2025, resulting in a program costing well over $1 trillion per year. Beyond that, as healthcare costs continue to increase and the bulk of the Boomer generation moves into retirement territory, it's anyone's guess as to where those numbers could go, or how the program could continue to be fully funded. For an explanation of why prices keep going up, see Chapter 12, "The Healthcare System."

PENSIONS

For those of you with a pension from your corporate or government employer, there's bad news: It is extremely unlikely that you'll see all of the payments and benefits promised to you. In fact, depending on when you retire and the state of your employer, it's very possible that you won't see anything at all.

The problem with pensions—especially "defined benefit" pensions, which guarantee a certain payment regardless of the performance of the pension fund's investments—is that they were popularized at a time when the world was very different. Like Social Security, they were introduced when people didn't live much past retirement, and they were designed by corporate and government leaders who wanted the immediate benefits without having to stick around to see the end game, so it was easy to make promises that future generations would have to fulfill.

As a wave of retirees hit the eligibility mark, and the expected returns on pension funds' investments fail to materialize, we're seeing the end game for these retirement promises.

Private Pensions

Private pensions are more than a century old—the first was offered in 1875—and are an artifact from an era when people would hold a job with a single employer for an extended time, often for their entire careers. While they are in decline (only 18 percent of corporate workers have them today, compared with 35 percent in the early 1990s)[75] because of the changing nature of the job market and because employers now have more retirement plan options available to them such as 401k programs, the fact remains that a large number of Americans receive, or expect to receive, support from these defined-benefit programs.

And they have some reason to expect that their pension plans will deliver on their promises: After some pension programs went bust in the 1960s due to a failure of employers to contribute as promised (the most notable case being the Studebaker auto plant), Congress passed a law in 1974 that set rules mandating that employers fund these programs, and established an insurance program through a new Pension Benefit Guaranty Corporation (PBGC) that takes over for failed pension programs.[76]

However, rules or no rules, corporations have had a hard time staying in business with the burden of these plans, and can shed them through bankruptcy or other restructurings. That's when the PBGC takes over. As of 2014, the organization has taken over 4,640 pensions covering more than 2.2 million retirees, with some of the biggest coming from the airline (Delta, Pan Am, United) and steel (Bethlehem, LTV, National) industries. As a result of its obligations, the PBGC was $61 billion in the red at the end of 2014.[77]

So, while the organization is currently able (despite its running deficit) to make the majority of people whole, or close to it, the future is less certain. Based on reports from private pension funds to the PBGC, they have seen the levels of funding among still-operating pensions drop from 84 percent in 2008 to 75 percent in 2014, putting the PBGC at risk of covering an additional $550 billion in obligations in a worst-case scenario.[78] Private pensions are clearly struggling, and the PBGC may soon be making some hard decisions on how to leverage its limited resources.

Government Pensions

Pensions for civil servants became popular at the same time as private pensions, when it was seen as a way to compensate government workers who received average to low pay.

And those pension plans are entering a crisis phase: Depending on who you ask, public pensions are underfunded by as little as $1.5 trillion (according to the Pew Charitable Trusts)[79] up to more than $5 trillion (according to a Pension Task Force established by the Actuarial Standards Board).[80] No matter which estimate you accept, the deficit in what pensions have versus what they have to pay out is staggering, and it's happened for three reasons:

- Outsized promises. Pension details vary widely by state, but as a rule pensions pay out much more than they take in from participants. Some are far more generous than others; California offers retirees a pension at 87 percent of what they were making as employees, with lifetime benefits approaching $1.3 million, while Mississippi offers retirees 54 percent of their former salaries, leading to average lifetime benefits of just $307,000.[81] And this is typically after thirty years of employment, resulting in people retiring in their fifties and living for thirty years or more.

- Underfunded systems. Politicians are typically very good at making promises, but very bad at following through. And as required payments to state pension systems become greater and greater, squeezing out other government priorities, many politicians have opted to delay or skip making those required payments, which will just compound funding problems in the future.[82]

- Unrealistic assumptions. In order to maintain the illusion that they'll be able to meet future obligations, most pension funds assume that they'll consistently make a fantastic return on their investments: Of 150 public pension funds surveyed, 97 percent assume that they'll make annual returns of between 7 and 8 percent.[83] Since low-risk investments don't provide anything like that (the 10-year Treasury bond is close to 2.5 percent as of this writing), many funds pursue risky investments in order to attempt to clear this bar.

While problems for public pensions were always considered to be in the future, there have been some recent developments indicating that the future is becoming today. Some towns, such as Stockton[84] and San Bernardino[85] in California, have been forced into bankruptcy due to their pension obligations. And some pension funds, such as the Central States Pension Fund[86] and the Dallas Police and Fire Pension System,[87] have either started talking about reducing benefits or halting lump-sum buyouts.

Whether you're relying on Social Security, pensions, or your own investments, the reality is that the stories you've been told about preparing for retirement have been just that: Stories. It's time to think about other ways to protect yourself in the future.

5

CAVEAT EMPTOR:
THE MONEY MASTERS

> History records that the money changers have used every
> form of abuse, intrigue, deceit, and violent means possible to
> maintain their control over governments by controlling
> money and its issuance.
>
> —James Madison

Let me be clear: I am not a financial advisor, have no particular
expertise in finance except as a consumer, and I am not licensed
or authorized to give anyone financial advice. What's more, I
generally don't like to tell anyone what to do: I want people to
gather their own information and make their own decisions. But
I will share some final thoughts that will hopefully help you in
your decision-making around money and finances.

GET OUT OF DEBT

If you want to be self-sufficient—if you want to stand as independent from the system as possible—the first thing you should do is
get rid of your debt as quickly as possible. When you owe someone, not only are you paying much more for the things you
bought, but you're generating huge profits for banks and other
financial firms. Consider how much they're making on your

credit cards: Banks are borrowing money from the Federal Reserve at an extremely low rate (approximately 1 percent at the time of this writing), and charging you an average interest rate of more than 16 percent on your unpaid credit card balance![88]

Don't let them have power over you. Do whatever it takes—earn more, spend less, or both—but start using any available funds to pay down and eliminate debt. Start with the highest interest debts first (probably your credit cards) and then tackle the larger ones, like your auto and home loans. Living debt-free is probably the single most empowering thing you can do.

DO BUSINESS WITH THOSE YOU TRUST

Banking, and financial services in general, is supposed to be a trust-based relationship. As noted in this chapter, big banks and financial firms have a documented history of breaking the law (sometimes in letter, sometimes in spirit) and bending the rules in their favor. Why would you want to do business with people like that? Before you decide to give someone your money, either for saving or investing, do your research to see if you think they're trustworthy. There are alternatives out there: Your community has many local options, including credit unions and community banks, that can provide for all your needs, for example.

LOOK FOR THE FEES

We all know that products and services cost money, including financial products, and I'll be the first to say that if a company provides me with value, they should get paid for that. But too often in the financial world, those fees are hidden or not disclosed. When you talk to an insurance broker, for example, he may give you insurance recommendations without telling you what his commission will be; since commissions can range from 2.7 percent to 14.3 percent on policies,[89] for example, he may be making recommendations that serve him better than they serve you. Or he may recommend a whole-life policy without telling you that more than half of the first year's premium ends up in his pocket.[90]

What's more, some business models are actually built on predatory practices, usually serving the most vulnerable communities. Consider payday lending, where you pay what seems like a small fee in order to get cash before your next paycheck. For example, you might write the payday lending company a check for $115, postdated by a week, in order to get $100 cash right now. People using this service typically do so as a last resort—they have no savings or other sources of funds—and often end up rolling over these loans, resulting in ballooning debts with an annual interest rate of 390 percent or more! [91]

LOOK FOR THE RISKS

There are regulations in place that require financial services companies to tell you about the risks associated with their products. Most people ignore that language; you shouldn't. Give careful thought to the risks involved in the financial products and services you buy, keeping in mind that the risks may be greater than what they're stating. (Specifically, because they don't reflect a lot of the issues outlined in this section of the book.) And realize that the veneer of stability presented by the financial industry is something of a false front: Consider, for example, how much banks emphasize that deposits are insured up to $250,000 by the FDIC, and then realize that the FDIC only has $67 billion in cash and Treasury bonds on hand[92] versus $11.4 trillion in total deposits in U.S. commercial banks.[93] Even though not all of those trillions in deposits are covered by the insurance (amounts over $250,000 aren't covered), it wouldn't take much of a bank run to exhaust those FDIC funds and leave your supposedly secure accounts in question.

BE PREPARED

We have a Federal Reserve completely winging it on monetary policy, and we have big financial institutions carrying far more risk than they did during the 2008 crisis. I think the possibility of short-term emergencies is real, and if you think it's possible as well, then it makes sense to insure yourself against that. Have some cash on hand—actual physical dollars, enough to cover two to three months of living expenses if possible. And think about some other ways of preparing for a short-term disruption, perhaps with food reserves and maybe even a little gold and silver on hand.

DON'T ASSUME THE WORST

That seems like an odd thought for a book like this. But the reality is, even if we're right in the long term, there's no telling what can happen in the short term, and how long reality can be avoided. If you pulled your money out of the market at the bottom of the crisis in 2008, you missed a near-tripling of the stock markets and a continued eight-year bull market in bonds. I can't tell you what's going to happen, or when, and neither can anybody else. The best strategy is probably that offered by Chuck Prince, former chairman of Citigroup: "As long as the music is playing, you've got to get up and dance."[94] Just keep a very watchful eye on the exit.

PART II

BIG GOVERNMENT

6

How you're getting screwed by . . .
POLITICIANS

Giving money and power to government is like giving whiskey and car keys to teenage boys.

—P.J. O'Rourke

THE POINT:

We vote for politicians, but they don't work for us—they work for big donors and lobbyists, whose interests rarely line up with ours, and for themselves. Politicians do this because they know there won't be any consequences: We'll reelect them anyway, and they won't be around to see the long-term impact of their actions.

A lot of people think the United States is a democracy. It isn't. The U.S. is a *republic*, in which we elect people who are supposed to represent our interests and work within the rule of law. And, while that system worked more or less for a very long time, it doesn't work anymore.

SERVING THE MANY, OR THE POWERFUL?

Politicians can talk a good game, but when it comes down to it, they vote based on what's best for the rich and powerful, not the masses or the country.

Remember the $700 billion bailout for the banks and insurance companies in 2008? Senator Barbara Boxer (CA) got more than 17,000 emails from constituents about it, almost all opposed. Senator Sherrod Brown (OH) said that of the 2,000 emails he had gotten, 95 percent were opposed.[95] The bailout bill passed anyway, of course, with both Boxer and Brown voting for it.[96]

Remember the Iraq War in 2003? Only 30 percent of Americans supported the use of military force;[97] most felt that diplomatic efforts had not been exhausted, and there still needed to be hard evidence justifying an attack. There were demonstrations worldwide against the launch of a campaign. Yet in we went.

These are just two examples; a paper from 2014, "Testing Theories of American Politics: Elites, Interest Groups, and Average Citizens,"[98] gives a more complete (and damning) picture. Professors from Princeton and Northwestern Universities looked at nearly 1,800 political decisions where the interests of the public were different from those of the powerful. They found that " . . . economic elites and organized groups representing business interests have substantial independent impacts on U.S. government policy, while average citizens and mass-based interest groups have little or no independent influence."

SHOW ME THE MONEY

If you want to know why politicians are so willing to ignore the citizens they serve, look no further than their campaign war chests. Politicians live and die on fundraising, and those who donate are the ones who get represented.

Let's take a look at the most recent (2016) hauls from the leaders of both parties, courtesy of data collected by the Center for Responsive Politics:[99]

	REPUBLICANS—HOUSE		REPUBLICANS—SENATE	
Title	Speaker	Majority Leader	Majority Leader	Majority Whip
Name	Paul Ryan	Kevin McCarthy	Mitch McConnell	John Cornyn
Total raised	$19.7MM	$7.7MM	$29.9MM	$15.8MM
Small Indiv.	0 percent	0 percent	4 percent	5 percent
Large Indiv.	30 percent	17 percent	58 percent	56 percent
PAC	8 percent	42 percent	21 percent	26 percent
Self-finance	0 percent	0 percent	6 percent	0 percent
Other	62 percent	40 percent	11 percent	13 percent

	DEMOCRATS—HOUSE		DEMOCRATS—SENATE	
Title	Minority Leader	Asst. Min. Leader	Minority Leader	Minority Whip
Name	Nancy Pelosi	James Clyburn	Charles Schumer	Dick Durbin
Total raised	$4.2MM	$2.2MM	$24.8MM	$10.3MM
Small Indiv.	43 percent	3 percent	2 percent	12 percent
Large Indiv.	25 percent	15 percent	74 percent	60 percent
PAC	28 percent	82 percent	19 percent	23 percent
Self-finance	0 percent	0 percent	0 percent	0 percent
Other	4 percent	0 percent	5 percent	4 percent

Only one of the leaders above gets a material amount of support from small individual donors ("small" is defined as giving $200 or less during the campaign cycle). All of them receive the majority of their funds from large donors and Political Action Committees, or PACs, which makes it clear to whom they're obligated.

TWO PARTIES, OR ONE?

People spend a tremendous amount of energy and money supporting their preferred political party. They feel passionately that members of their party are the good guys, and those in the other party are either evil, stupid, or wrong, or all of the above.

But are the two parties really that distinct? Or is this adversarial situation more of a distraction from other things?

Consider the following graphic:

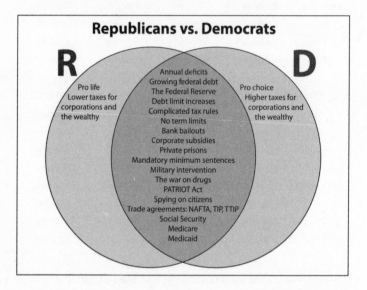

Republicans vs. Democrats

R

Pro life
Lower taxes for
corporations and
the wealthy

Annual deficits
Growing federal debt
The Federal Reserve
Debt limit increases
Complicated tax rules
No term limits
Bank bailouts
Corporate subsidies
Private prisons
Mandatory minimum sentences
Military intervention
The war on drugs
PATRIOT Act
Spying on citizens
Trade agreements: NAFTA, TIP, TTIP
Social Security
Medicare
Medicaid

D

Pro choice
Higher taxes for
corporations and
the wealthy

You can argue specifics here, and undoubtedly there are some additional differences, but the larger point is clear: These parties are not as different as you think, and they both dramatize their relatively small differences in order to feed you a false narrative, encourage you to pick a side, and allow you to overlook all the glaring problems of people wearing the same jersey as you.

When you back up, you can see that it's not really Democrats versus Republicans, it's liberty versus the state (with R's and D's both on the side of the state).

RULES FOR YOU, NOT FOR THEM

Politicians create rules and laws, but you might be surprised to learn that they also make sure that some of those rules don't apply to them.

As you might expect, the decisions that Congress makes can influence the stocks of individual companies as well as the stock market overall. Did you know that Congress made sure that insider trading laws didn't apply to them? They can make big bets on stocks, knowing in advance that their votes will cause those stocks to go up or down. And yes, Congress did remove that exemption in 2011 after an exposé on *60 Minutes*, but quietly rolled back many of the new reporting rules in 2013 (a non-election year).[100] Congress has also exempted itself from many of the workplace laws that the rest of us have to live by, such as whistleblower protection or keeping workplace safety records.[101]

This self-serving behavior extends to politicians' major donors and favored interest groups. Take the Affordable Care Act (ACA, or Obamacare) for example. Unions, a favored constituent of Democrats, received a waiver on fees tied to premium healthcare plans.[102]

You know those annoying robocalls? Congress made sure that companies can't call you anymore, but the government still can. As the *Washington Post* concluded, "Wherever you fall in this debate, the rules are clearer than ever: The government has a special status when it comes to blasting out phone calls to the public."[103]

This "special status" even filters down to their personal behaviors and attitudes. If Representative Nancy Pelosi wants to go shoe shopping, her driver can break traffic laws and park in front of a fire hydrant to get her there.[104] Senator Dianne Feinstein is one of the biggest supporters of the NSA's gathering information on the public, but is outraged when they go after her data.[105]

WHY DO THEY KNOW THEY CAN GET AWAY WITH IT?

How can they operate this way? Aren't they worried about the consequences? Actually they're not worried at all, for a few reasons.

Insufficient Representation

When government started operating under the rules of the Constitution (1789), there were only around 33,000 voters per congressman. There used to be a system to increase the number of congressmen as populations increased and new states joined the union, but in 1911 they passed a law that capped the number of people in congress, so the number of voters per congressman started to grow. In 2010, the ratio was around 710,000 voters per representative.[106]

You might have been able to communicate with, and influence, your representative when those numbers were small. But now? Forget it.

Redistricting

Based on the makeup of congressional districts, one of the two parties usually has a natural advantage—most have a larger number of Democrats than Republicans or vice versa. Today that has been taken to an extreme—computers have made it possible to figure out exactly where those lines should be drawn for maximum advantage, and as a result many districts are heavily lopsided in favor of one party or the other. In these districts, elections are usually decided at the primary stage (where big donors have an outsized influence), with the general election being practically a formality.

The Incumbent's Advantage

Remember Senators Boxer and Brown, who voted for the $700 billion bailout of the financial industry even though 95 percent or more of their voters were against it? They were both reelected. In fact, according to Politifact, politicians enjoy a 95 percent re-election rate,[107] even though only 9 percent of Americans have a "great deal" or "quite a lot" of trust in Congress.[108] It would be pretty hard to argue that their decisions or favorability ratings have any sort of consequences from the voting public.

We have a system rigged to get certain preselected people into office and keep them there, where they can work in the interests of the rich and the powerful—and we, the American public, vote them in based on the color of their jersey and keep them there no matter what they do. Is it any wonder they can do as they please while in office?

CASE STUDY: THE PRESIDENTIAL ELECTION

Every four years, we end up with a presidential election between one Democrat and one Republican. Each time, the politicians and the media tell us that "this is the most important election of our lives." Most of the population, on the other hand, has a different thought—namely, out of 330 million people, how did we end up with these two jokers as our only choices? It's not by accident. Actually, there are two reasons that our electoral system produces the poor choice that it does.

Primary Games

Admittedly, in 2016 Donald Trump broke almost every rule in politics, turning many of these challenges upside down. But in a normal elec-tion cycle, the election before the election—the primary season, when few members of the public are paying attention—determines who will represent each party in the general election.

And by most accounts, the primary system is a deeply flawed one, in which those who do pay attention—chiefly those who have some sort of interest in currying political favors, like donors and special interest groups—have an outsized impact on the results.

Money is the lifeblood of politics, and donors essentially choose who they think is both viable and palatable in their eyes; these favored candidates are the ones with the resources to compete in the primaries and make their way to the general. At the congressional level, for example, the better-funded candidate won his or her primary 83 percent of the time,[109] and the same impact is seen among presidential candidacies.

The order that states cast their primary ballots also influences the field; many times a candidate has already secured an insurmountable lead by March or April, leaving many states, such as California, without any voice in selecting the candidate.[110] Early support is doubly important on the Democratic side, where superdelegates provide critical votes that can counter the states' primary voters. In 2016, for example, Hillary Clinton walked away from more than a few states, such as New Hampshire, with more support even though Bernie Sanders ran away with the popular vote.

And don't forget the "inside baseball" element, where the national committees actually rig the outcomes behind the scenes. In 2016, Wikileaks revealed that the Democratic National Committee was explicitly favoring Clinton,[111] while in 2012, the Republican leadership changed convention rules at the last minute to prevent Ron Paul from receiving a nomination from his pledged delegates.[112]

Freezing Out Third Parties

Like most European countries, the United States has a number of political parties: In addition to the Democrats and Republicans, we have the Constitution Party, the Green Party, the Libertarian Party, and a long list of emerging and/or state-level parties.[113]

And yet when it comes to presidential elections, we almost always end up with a choice of either a Republican or Democrat—even in 2016, when the two parties put forth the most disliked candidates since such polling began.[114] This, of course, is by design: The two parties have worked hand in hand to keep others out of the presidential race.

First, it is extremely hard to get on the ballot in all 50 states, each of which has its own requirements for being included. And states tend to award their electoral votes based on an all-or-nothing system; in other words, if a candidate does well but doesn't claim outright victory, they will get no credit at all for their performance.[115]

Next, the presidential debates are a vital platform for reaching voters: Ralph Nader, Green Party candidate in 2000, regularly filled arenas, but said "in one debate I would have reached more people, by 50-fold, than I reached by filling all the major arenas."[116] But since 1987, the Commission on Presidential debates—a group founded through joint sponsorship by the Democratic and Republican national committees—has been the group to decide who participates, making it almost impossible for third party candidates to get on stage.

Finally, the media effectively shuts out third party candidates, denying them the ability to reach voters through mass channels unless they pay for the privilege. Academic Stephen Farnsworth, who conducted a study of third-party media coverage after the 2000 presidential campaign, said: "What's very clear is that reporters focus on the two major-party candidates. So if you're a third-party candidate and you don't possess the vast personal fortune of a Ross Perot, you're going to be ignored. Presidential candidates who do not have a D or R after their name are finished before they even start."[117]

For candidates who can't get into the debates, and can't get the media to cover them, there's one remaining path to mass awareness: Advertising. And here again, the big parties hold the advantage, with their huge donor bases, deep pockets, and access to lines of credit. In the 2016 election, Hillary Clinton spent $140 million on television ads through October 15, 2016, compared with Donald Trump's $40 million (lower due to the substantial amounts of free publicity he received throughout the campaign). These numbers are dwarfed by the $378 million spent by Barack Obama and the $472 million spent by Mitt Romney in the 2012 campaign. No word on what the independent candidates spent in these contests, but it was undoubtedly miniscule compared to the two-party heavyweights.[118]

Given the barriers to third parties, and the rigged primary process among the major parties, you can expect to continue to receive little choice in your presidential vote.

7

How you're getting screwed by . . .
THE GOVERNMENT

If you put the federal government in charge of the Sahara
Desert, in five years there'd be a shortage of sand.

—Milton Friedman

THE POINT:

The government is supposed to serve us. But more and more, it
serves itself, taking on more and more authority and keeping us in
the dark about what it's doing and what's really happening in our
country. It works for power over principles, including the principles
that are supposed to protect us as citizens.

When this country was founded, the federal government was
supposed to be a bare-bones support network for the member
states, just to do the things the states couldn't do themselves, like
raising an army or managing relationships with foreign countries. Now, the federal government is an out-of-control monster,
accountable to no one and focused on serving itself, not the
public.

Note that the examples below are literally just scratching the
surface; no book, no matter how long, could list all of the many

ways in which the government screws up, lies, and deceives the public.

FIGURES LIE, LIARS FIGURE

The federal government tracks a lot of different statistics, including everything from the unemployment rate to details on crime. We rely on them for honest information, but that's not always what we get. They've learned that if they publish positive information (whether or not there's any truth behind the numbers), the public is happier, complains less, and asks fewer questions.

A few examples:

GDP (Gross Domestic Product)

GDP is one of the most important and well-known numbers reported by the government. It's supposed to be a measure of economic growth—but because it is considered so important, it's hugely manipulated to make things look better than they are.

- Government spending is a component of the GDP; that means that if the government borrows money so it can spend more, we're artificially pumping up the GDP number with borrowed money. Think how much better GDP would be if we had a $2 trillion/year deficit, or $5 trillion.
- The government "adjusts" GDP based on things they pretend added value to the economy, even though no transactions actually took place. If you own your own home, for example, they figure out how much rent you would be paying yourself, and add that in. If you buy a $1,000 computer that has more features than the same computer last year, they add in more

than $1,000 to the GDP. Chris Martenson estimates that up to 35 percent of GDP is made up of these "hedonic" adjustments.[119]

- If they want to goose the GDP number, they'll count additional things in the formula. In 2013, for example, they were able to arbitrarily boost GDP by 3 percent instantly by including money earned from creative works including movies, television shows, books, theater, and music, as well as corporate research and development.[120]

Unemployment Rate

We know the economy is doing great because the unemployment rate is really low, right? Not so fast. This number, which comes from the Bureau of Labor Statistics (BLS), provides a completely inaccurate picture of the health of the economy, for the following reasons:

- It doesn't give you an accurate sense of how many people are out of work. There are several categories in the BLS report; the most commonly reported (U3) only reports on those who are unemployed and are actively looking for work. If people have been out of work for too long because they can't find a job, we stop counting them. Does that make sense?
- It tells you nothing about the quality of jobs, or who's getting them. A high-wage manufacturing job counts the same as a job at a fast-food joint. A part-time job counts as much as a full-time job. We can't tell that almost all the job gains are going to people over the age of 55 (true, by the way).[121]

- It uses a "fudge factor" called the Birth/Death Model, which adds in jobs they can't survey (like new business startups). Even though there are more business closures than there are startups these days,[122] the Birth/Death Model keeps adding tens or hundreds of thousands of jobs to the report.

Because the unemployment rate gets all the attention, it also gets manipulated the most. Other numbers, like the labor participation rate (a straight-up percentage of working-age people in the workforce), give a better picture of what's going on in this country. The labor participation rate in January 2016 was at 62.3 percent—the lowest level since 1978.[123]

The Deficit

The government is taking on debt at an alarming rate, and observers look at both the total debt (all that we owe) as well as the annual deficit (how much more we spent than we received in the past year). Every November, the government announces its deficit for the previous year. And every year they lie about its size.

Their announcement highlights the "official" deficit; but if you want the true number you need to calculate it from the Treasury Department's "Debt to the Penny" resource, where you can see exactly how much the government owed on October 1 of one year compared to the same date the next year. And the differences run into the hundreds of billions of dollars.

Fiscal year	Announced deficit (billions)[124]	Actual deficit (billions)[125]
FY 2016 (10/1/2015 to 9/30/2016)	616	1,423
FY 2015 (10/1/2014 to 9/30/2015)	438	275
FY 2014 (10/1/2013 to 9/30/2014)	485	1,077
FY 2013 (10/1/2012 to 9/30/2013)	680	579
FY 2012 (10/1/2011 to 9/30/2012)	1,087	1,276
FY 2011 (10/1/2010 to 9/30/2011)	1,300	1,179
FY 2010 (10/1/2009 to 9/30/2010)	1,294	1,641
FY 2009 (10/1/2008 to 9/30/2009)	1,413	1,786
FY 2008 (10/1/2007 to 9/30/2008)	459	962
FY 2007 (10/1/2006 to 9/30/2007)	161	501
Total deficit, 10 years, reported vs. actual	7,931	10,698[126]

Consumer Price Index (CPI)

According to the Bureau of Labor Statistics, the Consumer Price Index (CPI) is "a measure of the average change over time in the prices paid by urban consumers for a market basket of consumer goods and services."[127] It tracks things like food, apparel, housing, transportation, and other items commonly purchased by people as a way to track inflation.

The problem, however, is the CPI is the number government uses to adjust government benefits each year, including Social Security, federal retirement programs, inflation-protected securities (TIPs), salary and benefit increases, and more. So the government saves money when the CPI is low, which gives them a tremendous incentive to rig that number.

And the CPI, like many other government numbers, is heavily manipulated to get results the government wants. It is heavily influenced, for example, by hedonics, which means that if the price of steak rises, they will substitute the price of hamburgers, assuming people would make that switch. They over-represent the categories that don't show price increases, and underrepresent those that do. They won't share their raw data, making it impossible to audit their results. And what's more, over the past thirty years, the government has changed the way the CPI is calculated twenty times.[128]

As a result, according to one estimate, underweighting the CPI saved the government $150 billion, and possibly much more, between 1998 and 2012.[129] This savings was gained on the backs of those relying on the government to help them keep pace with inflation, including seniors and federal employees.

To get a sense of the real rate of inflation, you might consider the Chapwood Index, which provides straightforward reporting on "the actual price increase of the five hundred items on which most Americans spend their after-tax money" within the top fifty cities in the United States.[130] In 2014, for example, the CPI pegged inflation at 0.8 percent; the Chapwood Index, on the other hand, calculated inflation in cities ranging from Colorado Springs at 6.6 percent to San Jose at 13.7 percent.[131] Providing a more realistic calculation like this index would make the CPI more realistic; but of course it would also cost the government billions.

"The Recovery"

By my count, we've been talking about being in a recovery for more than six years. The first official statement on this came from Treasury Secretary Tim Geithner in an April 2010 editorial in the *New York Times*.[132] ("Welcome to the Recovery" caused a lot of laughter at the time, and still does.) Even before then, in 2009, the president of the Federal Reserve, Ben Bernanke, was talking about the "green shoots" that pointed to a coming rebound in the economy.[133]

But during the time they talked about that recovery, the economy for ordinary Americans has been fragile and weak; it never gets stronger, never gains momentum. We couldn't raise interest rates because the recovery was so fragile, and there are still millions of people struggling.

But why would they keep saying our "recovery" was so fragile? Is it because they were trying to make you think there was a recovery when there actually wasn't?

As financial website ZeroHedge notes, there's plenty of data that shows any semblance of a recovery is fiction. Student loans, food stamp usage, the federal debt, money printing, and health insurance costs are at record highs, while the labor force participation rate, workers' share of the economy, median family income, and home ownership rates are at or near multi-decade lows.[134]

SELF-PRESERVATION

As organizations get larger, they shift their focus from serving their missions to self-preservation. Government agencies certainly prove that point.

One example is how the government responds to Freedom of Information Act (FOIA) requests. Because the government is supposed to be working for us, we're supposed to have the right to see what they're doing, and we can do that by submitting FOIA requests. But lately the government hasn't wanted to share much: In 2015 they provided a complete response in only 23 percent of cases, and a partial response (with sections or complete documents missing) 40 percent of the time. There was no response at all 37 percent of the time.[135]

There are also scores of stories of governments covering up their mistakes rather than being honest and transparent. In one

Lifecycle of Bureaucracy

Dark=Program budget Light=Administrative costs

Expansion ➡️

Launch
*tight budgets
modest pay
minimal benefits
high camaraderie*

Growth
*rapid growth
in program
and staffing;
morale high*

Maturity
*"mission creep"
union & admin gain
political power; depts.
solidify, infighting*

Contraction ➡️

Bloat
*budget is flat but
admin costs rise;
gaming the system
and fraud are rife*

Budget Cuts
*program abandoned
as focus shifts to
protecting budget
and staff pay/benefits*

Failure/Implosion
*the competent retire
leaving the incompetent
in command; morale low,
chaos & failure the norm;
organizational implosion*

particularly bad case that began in 1990, a superintendent at Effigy Mounds National Monument in Iowa stole the museum's entire collection of human bones dug up from sacred Native American burial sites and stored them in his garage in "wildly inappropriate storage conditions." According to the AP, "A series of superintendents were warned that the museum's entire collection of human bones had gone missing under Munson, but they did little to find them and failed to notify affected tribes."[136]

Charles Hugh Smith notes a clear life cycle for bureaucratic organizations, in which they start small, with minimal overhead and most of their funds going to their mission (stage 1); going through phases where funding for both the mission and the bureaucracy grow; stages where funding declines, and the mission is sacrificed in favor of sustaining the bureaucracy; and ending in implosion, as an organization that exists solely to sustain itself. Government agencies are in the latter stages, headed towards the final event.[137]

HYPOCRISY

When there's something we want or need from other countries, our government cares more about keeping them happy than about upholding our principles and standards.

Saudi Arabia is supposedly one of our strongest allies in the Middle East. It's also a country that tortures and beheads a criminal every other day on average.[138] Women cannot obtain a passport, marry, travel, or access higher education without the approval of a male guardian. They do not allow public worship of any religion other than Islam.[139] Their laws punish acts of homosexuality or cross-dressing with death, imprisonment, fines, corporal punishment, or whipping/flogging.[140] And yet they're one of our strongest allies—all because of their oil and money. Are these friends you would want to have?

And what about China? They've taken a huge number of our manufacturing jobs, not because they're better at it but because they don't have the same worker rights or environmental standards that we have, making it much cheaper to operate there. The country is an environmental disaster, with severe water, air, and land pollution, largely caused by industry,[141] and workers have few rights and minimal pay.[142] Yet the U.S. gave them "Most Favored Nation" status in 1979, and has renewed that status every year since.[143]

Of course there's no shortage of hypocrisy on domestic issues either. After railing against deficits throughout President Obama's two terms, Republicans have now opened up the floodgates on military spending regardless of the impact on the bottom line. In fact, in September 2017, Senate Republicans voted to increase the defense budget by $81 billion in one year, taking it from $619 billion to $700 billion, in line with the House's increase of $77 billion.[144]

PROBLEMS THAT NEVER GET SOLVED

When problems become public knowledge, the government typically either papers over the problem or waits for it to fade from the headlines rather than actually fix anything.

The Transportation Security Administration, for example, is responsible for making sure terrorists can't get dangerous items onto aircraft. When an independent test revealed a 70 percent failure rate in 2005, people were understandably alarmed.[145] You would think that would cause them to make major changes, but it didn't, as proven by their 95 percent failure rate in 2015.[146]

How about the Veterans Administration, which is responsible for providing medical care for our military veterans? The agency has been under constant fire for decades due to poor service and multiple coverups.[147]

STEALING YOUR RIGHTS

Just as government assumes more and more rights beyond what was authorized in the Constitution, it has worked to take away the rights of its citizens. More power for them, less for you. You have fewer rights of expression and assembly (think about the "protest zones" that separate you from political conventions);[148] seizure of assets without any arrests, even including pulling money from your debit cards;[149] warrantless spying on citizens by the National Security Administration;[150] and so much more, far more than we can cover here.

Those asset seizures, otherwise known as "Civil Asset Forfeitures," are especially outrageous. In a country where people are supposed to be innocent until proven guilty, Civil Asset Forfeiture allows law enforcement to take your assets if they think they have been used in, or resulted from, criminal activity. No proof is required: An officer only has to say he or she suspects, and they can take your cash, vehicle, or other assets immediately. This action affects the poor the most—the people with the most to lose, and least able to hire an attorney to sue for their assets back. As Supreme Court Justice Thomas noted in a blistering statement on the topic:

> According to one nationally publicized report, for example, police in the town of Tenaha, Texas, regularly seized the property of out-of-town drivers passing through and collaborated with the district attorney to coerce them into signing waivers of their property rights. In one case, local officials threatened to file unsubstantiated felony charges against a Latino driver and his girlfriend and to place their children in foster care unless they signed a waiver. In another, they seized a black plant worker's car and all his property (including cash he planned to use

for dental work), jailed him for a night, forced him to sign away his property, and then released him on the side of the road without a phone or money. He was forced to walk to a Wal-Mart, where he borrowed a stranger's phone to call his mother, who had to rent a car to pick him up.[151]

This is not a small problem, or a set of isolated cases: The *Washington Post* reported that in 2015, these asset seizures surpassed the total losses from all burglaries in 2015. And it's a strategy that the incoming Attorney General, Jeff Sessions, has embraced, rolling back the limited reforms put in place by the Obama administration.[152] Unless Congress takes action, we should expect to see it continue well into the future.

LYING TO YOU

Few of us trust government in general, or politicians in particular. And it may be small comfort to know that the government had a law against domestic propaganda, passed in 1948, to supposedly ensure that our propaganda efforts were only to be used overseas. It will surely be less comfort to know that this law, the Smith-Mundt Act, was repealed in 2013, making it legal to disseminate propaganda within the borders of the United States.[153]

To make things worse, in light of the histrionics about Russian influence in the U.S. election, you might be surprised to learn that Congress recently slipped even more aggressive language, the Countering Foreign Propaganda and Disinformation Act of 2016, into a larger bill to fund intelligence activities, specifically H.R. 6393, the Intelligence Authorization Act for Fiscal Year 2017. This frightening piece of legislation takes us all the way back to the cold war, with authority and funding that "will improve the ability of the United States to counter foreign propaganda and disinformation by establishing an interagency center housed at the State Department to coordinate and synchronize counter-propaganda efforts throughout the U.S. government."[154] In other words, not only does the government no longer have any restrictions on domestic propaganda, it is now actively funding such efforts and ensuring that these activities are coordinated across agencies.

The bottom line is that the government, which was designed to be a servant to the people, is rapidly becoming the master. And our rights, and our freedom as citizens, are suffering as a result.

8

How you're getting screwed by . . .
THE MILITARY

War is a racket. It always has been. It is possibly the oldest, easily the most profitable, surely the most vicious. It is the only one international in scope. It is the only one in which the profits are reckoned in dollars and the losses in lives.

—Smedley D. Butler, *War Is a Racket*

THE POINT:

We spend tremendous amounts on our military—more than any other country by far—and are rewarded with never-ending wars that most of us would not support, managed by a system that has misspent trillions of dollars and lost billions in equipment in war zones. The military does not deserve our blind patriotism, but instead a watchful and skeptical eye on what they do in our names.

Let's be clear: Serving your country in the armed services is an honorable thing to do and, just as you wouldn't hold a bank teller responsible for the behavior of his CEO, you cannot hold rank and file soldiers responsible for the orders their military and political leaders give or the decisions they make. When we talk about the military here, we're speaking specifically of those decision-makers and how they use the armed forces to accomplish their own goals, whether or not they serve the rest of us.

And if we're not afraid to be honest—not worried about people calling us "unpatriotic" for questioning the military's actions, just as we question the actions of every other part of government—we can admit that the military is not being deployed in ways that serve our country.

We can admit that politicians use the military in ways that have nothing at all to do with our nation's security. We can admit that corporations are generating blockbuster profits at our expense. And we can admit that the call to patriotism blinds us to the fact that the military is host to some of the most incompetent, spendthrift leaders in the world.

HOW BIG IS OUR MILITARY?

How often have you heard politicians talking about "restoring our military," acting as if they've faced steep budget cuts and are

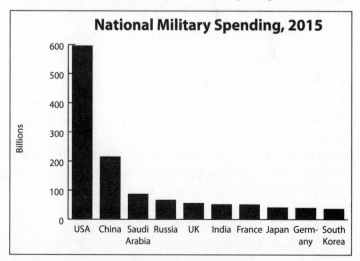

National Military Spending, 2015

starved for resources? It's a safe political rallying cry, but it's nowhere close to the truth. The fact is, our military is the largest in the world by far.

Consider how much we spend on our military compared to other countries: The U.S., at $596 billion in 2015, spends more on its military than the next seven countries combined ($567.2 billion).[155]

We also have the second-largest military in terms of soldiers currently serving, with 1.5 million active duty personnel as of 2014. Only China has more, with 2.3 million currently serving there.[156]

Our funding and size allows us to maintain a sprawling global network of approximately eight hundred military bases; in comparison, Britain, France, and Russia have a combined total of thirty foreign bases.[157] Many of our bases are in affluent, first-world countries simply because we fought wars there decades ago, including 174 in Germany, 113 in Japan, and 83 in South Korea.[158] The rest are scattered around the world, from Antigua to the United Kingdom.[159]

MILITARY ENGAGEMENTS—AN HONEST ASSESSMENT

Why do we invest so much in our armed forces? With the exception of Mexico and Canada, we are separated from the rest of the world by great distance, making a war on American soil unlikely. In fact, with the exception of the Pearl Harbor attack in Hawaii, there has been no foreign military attack of any substance on U.S. soil in the past hundred years.

The government tells us that all of this spending is for our protection—to defend our country, to defend our way of life. In fact, they even changed the name of the military institution from

the "War Department" to the "Department of Defense" in 1947
to reinforce that idea.[160]

But the wars that we've fought have been wars of choice. Most
people will find some of those, like World Wars I and II, to be
justifiable, despite the tremendous cost in terms of money and
lives: We were coming to the aid of longstanding allies who had
asked for our help. But the majority of our military adventures,
both before and after these world wars, have involved advancing
American interests, as opposed to defending ourselves or our
allies. "Might makes right" became our motto—diplomacy at the
end of a gun. And while most of us are probably comfortable
with the idea of the military defending our country, I doubt that
nearly as many would agree with using our military to force others to bend to our will in international matters.

The terrorist attack of September 11, 2001 seems to be a particular turning point—the moment at which we decided to wage
war on numerous countries, despite the fact that none had
attacked us. As former General Wesley Clark noted in a 2007
interview on *Democracy Now*:

> I had been through the Pentagon right after 9/11. About ten
> days after 9/11, I went through the Pentagon and I saw Secre-
> tary Rumsfeld and Deputy Secretary Wolfowitz. I went down-
> stairs just to say hello to some of the people on the Joint Staff
> who used to work for me, and one of the generals called me in.
> He said, "Sir, you've got to come in and talk to me a second." I
> said, "Well, you're too busy." He said, "No, no." He says, "We've
> made the decision we're going to war with Iraq." This was on or
> about the 20th of September. I said, "We're going to war with
> Iraq? Why?" He said, "I don't know." He said, "I guess they
> don't know what else to do." So I said, "Well, did they find some

information connecting Saddam to al-Qaeda?" He said, "No, no." He says, "There's nothing new that way. They just made the decision to go to war with Iraq." He said, "I guess it's like we don't know what to do about terrorists, but we've got a good military and we can take down governments." And he said, "I guess if the only tool you have is a hammer, every problem has to look like a nail."

So I came back to see him a few weeks later, and by that time we were bombing in Afghanistan. I said, "Are we still going to war with Iraq?" And he said, "Oh, it's worse than that." He reached over on his desk. He picked up a piece of paper. And he said, "I just got this down from upstairs"—meaning the Secretary of Defense's office —"today." And he said, "This is a memo that describes how we're going to take out seven countries in five years, starting with Iraq, and then Syria, Lebanon, Libya, Somalia, Sudan and, finishing off, Iran."[161]

The focus of our military adventures has changed since that list was shared with General Clark, possibly because it seems that we've been unable to achieve anything of significance in Afghanistan and Iraq, even after one and a half decades. But we have been active nonetheless: We did turn Libya into a failed state thanks to our support of insurgents and an associated bombing campaign,[162] and we have worked for years to destabilize Syria and encourage regime change, though Russia's involvement has turned the tide in the government's favor. In fact, President Obama became the first president in history to be at war for every day of his eight-year term,[163] and we dropped more than 26,000 bombs in seven different countries just in 2016:[164]

Syria	12,192
Iraq	12,095
Afghanistan	1,337
Libya	496
Yemen	34
Somalia	14
Pakistan	3
Total	26,172

Why? Why have we invested so much in our military, and why are we almost constantly instigating military action against supposedly sovereign countries? The answer to those questions can be found in the pockets of corporations and bankers.

ALL WARS ARE BANKER WARS

For people who lend money, and people who sell things to the military, war can be an immensely profitable activity. In his landmark book, *War Is a Racket*, Smedley Butler, one of the most decorated Marines in American history, reflected back on his military career only to realize that all of his actions were done for the benefit of American corporations overseas, and had nothing to do with protecting the country or preserving American ideals.

Politicians are natural advocates for military growth and spending: In the public's eyes, support for the military is patriotism personified, and members of Congress benefit greatly from the military spending that takes place in their districts, either from military personnel on bases or from the defense contractors and their suppliers who hire people and pay taxes. It doesn't hurt that politicians receive big donations from defense firms—$74 million in lobbying in 2015 alone.[165] That may help to explain why politicians are so supportive of military spending that they actually pass legislation forcing the military to buy things they don't even want, such as the hundreds of millions of dollars allocated to the purchase of Abrams tanks that the military has repeatedly said it doesn't want.[166]

Defense firms obviously benefit from military spending, and in addition to direct political lobbying, one of the ways that they push for more spending and larger contracts is to hire people directly from the field. Mid-level and upper-level military leaders know that if they want a career in industry when they retire from the service, they had better build up some relationships now.[167]

MILITARY MISMANAGEMENT

When people think of the military, most think of young, clean-cut men and women in uniform engaged in drills or going into battle. Few probably think about the service members sitting behind a desk, balancing the books. But there is a saying that an army marches on its stomach, and for an army that relies on funding to do its work, that role is nearly as important.

Unfortunately, it's a role that the military has proven completely incapable of fulfilling. On September 10, 2001, the day before the attacks on the World Trade Center and the Pentagon, Secretary of Defense Donald Rumsfeld admitted that the Pentagon could not track $2.3 trillion in spending.[168] Several years later, in 2016, the Pentagon announced a much larger number: $6.5 trillion in erroneous adjustments to their books.[169] Weeks later, they made an additional announcement—that they had identified $125 billion in wasteful spending on administration.[170] Simply put, the Pentagon's financial systems are so bad they have no ability to correctly track what they're spending.

To make matters worse, they have a bad habit of losing matériel in war zones, such as $420 million worth of weapons systems, vehicles, encryption devices, and communications gear in Afghanistan in 2014,[171] and then the next year more than $500 million in military aid in Yemen.[172]

To sum up, we spend more on our military than any other country in the world; use that military for purposes that most Americans would not agree with; and do a tremendously poor job of managing our resources. The citizens who pay for these military misadventures, long kept in the dark about all of this, have a right to know how their money is being used and misused here.

9

How you're getting screwed by . . .
THE EDUCATION SYSTEM

Schools teach exactly what they are intended to teach and they do it well: How to be a good Egyptian and remain in your place in the pyramid.

—John Taylor Gatto, *Dumbing Us Down*

THE POINT:

At one time, the education system in this country served to bring a nation together with a common culture and to prepare them to take on the responsibilities of adulthood. But today, the public schools have lost their purpose, an example of form over function, while higher education leaves you deep in debt and unprepared for the future.

K-12: DISCONNECTED

Looking back, do you feel like school prepared you for life? Did high school prepare you for college? Did either high school or college prepare you for work? Did they give you the practical skills to live independently?

Most people would say no to those questions. The obvious question, then, is why not? We know for a fact that every single person who goes from kindergarten through grade 12 is going to become an adult who will need to live independently and probably start a career. Wouldn't you think that the whole point of school would be to prepare people for what we absolutely know is going to happen?

When the public school system was created, it had a clear dual purpose: Give a nation of unskilled immigrants a shared identity as Americans, and give them the basic skills they needed to succeed in the workplace.

However, as Neil Postman noted in *The End of Education: Redefining the Value of School*, our current school model has not had a sense of purpose for some time. We have abandoned our shared narrative as Americans—we are no longer building a public. And we no longer focus on building practical life and work skills, save for a narrow band of instruction focused on career and technical education. As Scott London notes in his review of Postman's book, "At the moment, he says, education is geared toward economic utility, consumerism, technology, multiculturalism, and other bogus objectives. Narratives such as these are incapable of providing a rich and sustaining rationale for public education."

COMMON CORE, AND OTHER MISGUIDED REFORMS

When a system doesn't have a purpose (or ignores what should be its purpose), then you can come up with lots of false goals to target, and lots of false solutions to "help." Common Core is one of those false solutions: It was written at the urging of big business (Bill Gates[173] was key here),[174] run through the National Governors Association to give it respectability, and forced on schools across the country by Arne Duncan.

There were only five people involved in writing the standards; none were classroom teachers, and two had never done standards work before. There were sixty participants on the review committees, only one of whom was a practicing classroom teacher.[175] Two on that committee, Dr. Sandra Stotsky (language arts) and Dr. James Milgram (math), have refused to endorse the finished product and have in fact written and testified against those standards repeatedly.[176] And analysis after the fact shows that the standards do not prepare students for STEM, nor do they make them college and career ready.[177]

And yet, due to the political pressure of the National Governors Association and funding incentives from the Department of Education, almost all states adopted the new standards (though some have backed away due to parent pushback). Note that they had never been tried out anywhere: We forced a new set of learning standards on more than 50 million children without any proof at all that they had value. This is just one example of the kind of wrong-headed and even damaging reform that comes from not having a clear purpose.

COLLEGE FOR ALL

Almost all high school students are told that success in life requires a four-year college degree. For many of them, that's really bad advice.

The idea, like most in education, started with good intentions: College graduates tend to earn more, and have a lower unemployment rate, than those who don't have a college degree. But to say that everyone should get a degree, and will then enjoy those advantages, is just flawed logic.

First is the supply and demand issue: If we have an oversupply of college graduates, wages will go down, and a lot of those people with college degrees (and the student loans that go with them) will end up in jobs that don't need a degree. And that's already happening. In 1970, for example, only 5 percent of retail clerks had a college degree; in 2010 that was 25 percent. In 1970, 1 percent of cab drivers had a college degree; that is now 15 percent.[178]

Second, while more and more jobs require degrees, they're not necessarily four-year degrees. Lots of jobs, particularly hands-on jobs, require two year degrees or certifications, both of which cost a lot less and still lead to jobs that pay well and have a lot of job security. Examples include diagnostic medical sonographer (median annual salary: $64,280), paralegal ($49,500), respiratory therapist ($58,670), and electrician ($52,720).[179] And finally, in high-poverty communities where many students are struggling with basic skills, imposing a college-prep curriculum almost guarantees poor outcomes, like high dropout rates, without actually increasing the number of poor students who get a college degree.[180] In fact, only eight percent of low-income children in America earn a bachelor's degree by their mid-twenties, compared to more than 80 percent of students from the top income quartile.[181]

PRICE OF COLLEGE

A lot of people consider education, particularly college education, to be an investment in your future. That may or may not be true; but what we do know is that this investment has gotten more and more expensive over the years.

According to official sources, the cost of attending a four-year public college went up 250 percent between 1982 and 2012;[182] that number, with inflation, is nearly 600 percent![183]

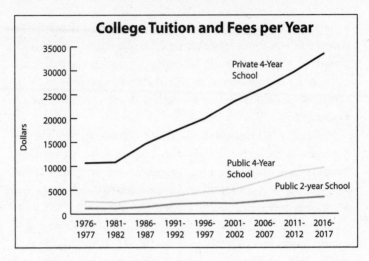

There's no one reason for this; rather there are a lot of contributing factors, like increasing demand for seats, increased services from colleges, reduced public funding for colleges, and freely-available student loans (more on that in the next section). But regardless of the reason or reasons, the fact that college costs have gone up so much, when incomes and job prospects have not, means that a lot of people will be getting degrees that won't benefit them, coupled with a heavy debt burden they will carry for years.

STUDENT LOANS

With college prices going up so fast, and family incomes not keeping pace, there was no way that most families could save up enough money to cover those costs themselves. That's where student loans come in.

People have borrowed money for college for decades, both through loans from the federal government and from private banks, which were then guaranteed by the federal government. But in 2010, the government forced private banks out of that business, saying there was no benefit to consumers, and now makes all student loans itself.[184]

Student loans have continued to grow quickly; today people owe more than $1.3 trillion in student loans as shown in the chart below,[185] which works out to an average debt of $29,000.[186]

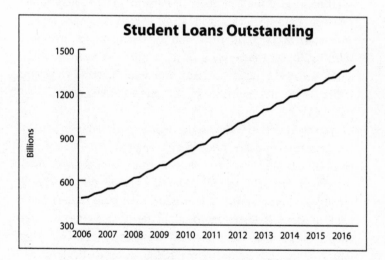

This causes all kinds of problems. First, one in four of those loan holders is struggling to make their payments or are already in default.[187] And those loans weigh heavily on the economy as a whole: They've been noted as a reason for the reduced number of business startups, lower levels of home ownership, marrying later in life, and postponing the decision to have children.[188]

And the kicker? Thanks to lobbying by the financial industry, congress passed "The Bankruptcy Abuse Prevention and Consumer Protection Act," which says that you can't get rid of student loan debt through bankruptcy.[189] Once you take out a student loan, you'll either pay it back or carry that debt forever.

FOR-PROFIT COLLEGES

For-profit colleges have been around since Colonial times, and had such early advocates as Benjamin Franklin. But when John Sperling opened the University of Phoenix in 1976, his unconventional model, which included course credit for work experience and, in 1989, an early and aggressive move to online learning, allowed for rapid growth. Within five years of going public (in 1994), the school had a hundred thousand enrollees. Other for-profit schools, seeing Phoenix's success, began to go public as well.[190]

For many of these schools, the rapid growth required of public companies quickly resulted in compromised quality and hard-sell enrollment efforts. Degrees from these colleges, even those with national accreditation, are not always considered credible with employers,[191] and in many cases leave students ineligible to pursue industry certifications, despite glowing promises about industry placement rates and the promise of high-paying jobs. And they use aggressive marketing tactics particularly targeted at vulnerable populations and people exiting the military, who are particularly attractive targets because the G.I. Bill still allows funds to be used at these colleges.[192]

While not all for-profit colleges are deceptive—some of the worst actors have been shut down in recent years, and federal funding guidelines have been tightened to reduce the incentive for fraud—anyone seeking an education should do a great deal of due diligence before committing their time and money to one of these schools.

Whether at the secondary or postsecondary levels, the true purpose of the American education system seems to be to make sure children are unprepared for the adult world—and to charge them huge sums for the privilege.

10

CAVEAT EMPTOR: BIG GOVERNMENT

> When government fears the people, there is liberty. When the people fear the government, there is tyranny.
>   —Unknown; often attributed to Thomas Jefferson

The author G. K. Chesterton said that "America is the only nation in the world that is founded on a creed." We were founded on the idea that the individual, by his or her very existence, has certain rights that cannot be taken away—that as long as we don't attempt to impact the rights of others, we are free to live our lives in any way we want.

The country's founding document—the Declaration of Independence[193]—lays this groundwork right from the start of the second paragraph: "We hold these truths to be self-evident, that all men are created equal, that they are endowed by their Creator with certain unalienable Rights, that among these are Life, Liberty and the pursuit of Happiness. That to secure these rights, Governments are instituted among Men, deriving their just powers from the consent of the governed . . . "

In other words, we have rights that cannot be taken away, and the only reason to have a government is to make sure those rights are protected. We are not here to serve government; government is here to serve us.

But over the years, with a slow and constant drip, government has grown larger and larger, and it has imposed upon those supposedly unalterable rights with greater and greater force. As a result, your personal freedoms have been limited. You are no longer free in the sense that your parents, grandparents, and those before them were free. And it's important to recognize that, and to know what to do about it.

OH, HOW FAR WE HAVE COME . . .

The Constitution of the United States is in many ways an operations guide, discussing how government is supposed to function. Out of a sense of concern of government imposing on the rights of its citizens, the Founding Fathers also took the time to draft a Bill of Rights[194] that lays out, in practical terms, some of the ways in which our rights must be respected.

There are 27 Amendments in the Bill of Rights, with ten passed initially and another 17 added in later years. While there are some important rights recognized in the later Amendments, such as women's right to vote, the original ten are usually considered as the essential listing of the fundamental ways in which the government must respect our rights.

An important note: There's a big difference between government restricting your rights and private companies banning certain activities. If a government makes it illegal to talk about something, that's a violation of your rights; if a private newspaper refuses to publish your article, that is their right since they can choose how they want to conduct their business. Don't pretend that your rights have been violated if a private company refuses to let you use their resources in any way you choose.

Amendment I

Congress shall make no law respecting an establishment of religion, or prohibiting the free exercise thereof; or abridging the freedom of speech, or of the press; or the right of the people peaceably to assemble, and to petition the Government for a redress of grievances.

One of the most fundamental expressions of our innate rights as citizens is the ability, and the responsibility, to say what we think; it's also one of the greatest dangers to a political establishment that wishes to keep growing in size and power. For this reason, our right to speak, what we want and where we want, is under increasing attack.

Consider, for example, how dissenting thought is treated in our public education system, particularly on college campuses. Conservative college professors are outnumbered by liberals at a 12 to 1 ratio,[195] and most feel they have to hide their beliefs to avoid being discriminated against.[196] They face challenges in getting published—a key activity for those wishing to advance—and can find getting tenure to be harder.[197] And students have effectively worked to banish dissenting opinions, making sure conservative guest speakers were disinvited from appearances,[198] demanding "safe spaces" free of contrary points of view, and even calling police or campus security when students share their beliefs or openly pray.[199]

Things aren't much better off-campus. We need permits to hold a protest, and our major political parties go so far as to fence off "free speech zones" far from their debates and conventions to remove protestors from their activities.[200] And the constant surveillance of citizens conducted by the NSA, made possible by the Patriot Act, gives us all pause when thinking about who we associate with and what we say.[201]

The idea that "I disapprove of what you say, but I will defend to the death your right to say it," words penned by Beatrice Evelyn Hall to describe Voltaire's thoughts, are shared by fewer and fewer people in today's America.

Amendment II

A well regulated Militia, being necessary to the security of a free State, the right of the people to keep and bear Arms, shall not be infringed.

In spite of this Amendment's clear wording, there are thousands of laws and regulations at the federal, state, and local levels that limit people's right to have guns. If you want a gun you'll probably have to submit to a background check, wait for several days before receiving a gun you bought, and face a number of limits on carrying and using that gun, such as various concealed carry laws and restrictions on where you can bring your gun.

I understand people's desire for wanting to restrict guns to make the world a safer place, but the facts run counter to that solution. The *Washington Post*, for example, found no correlation (and technically, a slightly negative correlation) between a state's homicide rate and how restrictive their gun control laws are.[202] And in terms of mass shootings, the *National Review* notes that, "Since at least 1950, all but two public mass shootings in America have taken place where general citizens are banned from carrying guns. In Europe, there have been no exceptions."[203]

Others argue that the Founders never envisioned modern technology like Uzi submachine guns and rocket launchers. But that's irrelevant. The Amendment was written not so that we would have firearms for hunting and sport shooting, but to defend ourselves and preserve our freedom. Remember that the Founders had just overthrown an unjust government, and they fully expected that despite the protections they put in the Constitution and Bill of Rights, that future citizens might need to do the same. The right to bear arms ensures that a future unjust government cannot force us to disarm, keeping us powerless. As the Declaration of Independence states, "whenever any Form of Government becomes destructive of [our rights], it is the Right of the People to alter or to abolish it, and to institute new Government . . . "[204] and the right to bear arms was intended to make sure we had the resources to do so if needed.

Finally, for those who would insist that this Amendment is no longer relevant, and that gun restrictions are warranted, remember that there is a procedure in place to repeal or amend the Bill of Rights: We've added multiple Amendments since the first 10 were enacted, and even repealed one (Prohibition). So if you find it outdated, work to change it; don't just ignore it.

Amendment III

No Soldier shall, in time of peace be quartered in any house, without the consent of the Owner, nor in time of war, but in a manner to be prescribed by law.

One spot of good news: The government isn't forcing us to house soldiers. Of course, with an annual budget of nearly $600 billion,[205] housing at least shouldn't be a problem.

Amendment IV

The right of the people to be secure in their persons, houses, papers, and effects, against unreasonable searches and seizures, shall not be violated, and no Warrants shall issue, but upon probable cause, supported by Oath or affirmation, and particularly describing the place to be searched, and the persons or things to be seized.

Few Amendments have been violated as thoroughly and consistently as the Fourth Amendment. In essence, this law protects our right to privacy, saying that it cannot be violated unless there is probable cause—some kind of evidence—that a crime has been committed, and even then, warrants that are issued to pursue additional evidence must be narrowly constructed and consistent with the allegation.

And yet, thanks to an intrusive spy network, recent legislation like the terrorist-hunting Patriot Act, and ever-increasing levels of sophistication in technology, we see that the government is vacuuming up as much data on each of us as they can. Edward Snowden revealed the scope of the NSA's efforts to collect data on all of our phone calls and emails,[206] just months after Director of National Intelligence James Clapper lied to Congress, saying that no such efforts were taking place.[207] (And no, he has not been indicted or punished for lying under oath.) We know that the FISA court, a secret court that decides on warrants requested by spy agencies, is a rubber-stamp outfit, rejecting just 0.03 percent of such requests as of 2013.[208] We even have spy planes as a constant presence circling over cities like Baltimore, recording everything that happens below through an array of cameras with cutting edge lenses and scopes.[209] It's hard to imagine what else the government could do to further intrude on the rights highlighted by this Amendment.

Amendment V

No person shall be held to answer for a capital, or otherwise infamous crime, unless on a presentment or indictment of a Grand Jury, except in cases arising in the land or naval forces, or in the Militia, when in actual service in time of War or public danger; nor shall any person be subject for the same offence to be twice put in jeopardy of life or limb; nor shall be compelled in any criminal case to be a witness against himself, nor be deprived of life, liberty, or property, without due process of law; nor shall private property be taken for public use, without just compensation.

This Amendment gives protection to those accused, but not yet convicted, of a crime: A grand jury must find that a trial is worthwhile; you cannot be tried twice for the same crime; you cannot be forced to testify against yourself; and your rights cannot be restricted, nor your property confiscated, while you're still only a suspect.

And yet there's a growing sense today that people are guilty until proven innocent. In *Salinas v. Texas*, the Supreme Court actually ruled that a man had no right to remain silent unless he specifically stated that right; otherwise his silence could be used to indicate guilt, and that could be used against him.[210] Police are using "civil asset forfeiture" to take money and property from people if they think those items are connected to crime, with millions of dollars being seized each year and often being funneled directly into police department budgets. According to the *Washington Post*, as of 2014, police had seized $2.5 billion in cash without search warrants or indictments since 2001.[211] And don't forget about the government's "no fly" list, in which people suspected of being terrorists (again, without formal accusation or charge) are denied the ability to fly and, in some cases, purchase guns. People are not notified that they're on the list, and the appeals process is (likely intentionally) very difficult to navigate.[212]

Amendment VI

In all criminal prosecutions, the accused shall enjoy the right to a speedy and public trial, by an impartial jury of the State and district wherein the crime shall have been committed, which district shall have been previously ascertained by law, and to be informed of the nature and cause of the accusation; to be confronted with the witnesses against him; to have compulsory process for obtaining witnesses in his favor, and to have the Assistance of Counsel for his defence.

The standards established by this Amendment are largely still respected; however, there have been numerous examples of people waiting for excessive periods for trials, particularly when a lack of public defenders forces defendants to wait months or even years for their trial.[213] Further, public defenders have developed a reputation, not without cause, for pushing defendants to accept plea deals, sometimes even when they're innocent.[214] And in times of national emergency, such as war, this Amendment and others are conveniently ignored. Consider the case of Japanese citizens and residents being forced into internment camps during World War II, leading to violations of several Amendments including this one.

Amendment VII

In Suits at common law, where the value in controversy shall exceed twenty dollars, the right of trial by jury shall be preserved, and no fact tried by a jury, shall be otherwise re-examined in any Court of the United States, than according to the rules of the common law.

This Amendment is more or less intact; the only encroachment has been with the idea of forced arbitration, in which contracts state that legal disputes will be solved privately, denying a plaintiff access to a trial by jury. These clauses are being written more and more often into the terms of agreement with corporations, such as credit card agreements and agreements for retirement accounts.[215]

Amendment VIII

Excessive bail shall not be required, nor excessive fines imposed, nor cruel and unusual punishments inflicted.

When people talk about this Amendment, they usually gravitate towards the issue of the death penalty, and people of good conscience can disagree on this topic. But what seems to be a much clearer issue are the excessive sentences brought about over the past 30 years, with rules that remove any discretion from the hands of the judges issuing sentences.

Consider the "Three Strikes" laws found around the country, where people who commit a crime with two previous convictions of any kind will find themselves at the receiving end of long sentences. In California, Curtis Wilkerson stole a pair of socks from a Mervyn's department store in 1995 and ended up with a life sentence.[216] Or consider the punishments for drug possession brought about by our nation's "war on drugs." While the federal government and states are now easing treatment of drug offenders, the rules of the last few decades have put thousands into prison—around half of the nation's 200,000 federal inmates are there for drug-related convictions—and sentenced them in many cases to decades of incarceration even for first-time offenses.[217]

And in terms of imposing excessive fines, private companies have been allowed to insert themselves into the legal process in ways that severely impact defendants. In Craigshead County, Arkansas, a private company manages the local probation process. Those who cannot pay the fines associated with their probationary sentence find new fees and fines piling up quickly, with the threat of jail used for enforcement. For hundreds of people, fines of as low as a few hundred dollars have morphed into debts of $10,000 or more; as the Marshall Project notes, this represents "an amount these defendants had no hope of repaying, and an amount orders of magnitude greater than the fines set forth by statute."[218]

Amendment IX

The enumeration in the Constitution, of certain rights, shall not be construed to deny or disparage others retained by the people.

This Amendment makes it clear that the government does not grant us rights; we have those rights as Americans, they predate the government and exist independently of it. The Bill of Rights simply recognizes some of them, and is not intended to deny other expressions of our individual rights.

Amendment X

The powers not delegated to the United States by the Constitution, nor prohibited by it to the States, are reserved to the States respectively, or to the people.

This Amendment says that the federal government cannot do anything that's not specifically assigned to it in the Constitution. And yet the federal government has grown to involve itself in just about everything you can think of. There's nothing at all about education in the Constitution, for example, yet we have a cabinet-level Department of Education effectively dictating agenda and policy. They get around this by making participation in all these programs and policies "voluntary," tying them to funding incentives—saying that if you want this $3 billion in education funding, you have to do things the way we want them done. The fact remains, however, that states were intended to serve as laboratories of democracy, each trying different things to see what worked best, rather than have a deep-pocketed overseer dictating things to all.

It's clear from the examples above that governments are actively intruding on our rights as citizens, and that the process will continue if we don't push back.

SHOULD YOU GET INVOLVED IN GOVERNMENT?

When you see so much corruption and dysfunction in government, there's a temptation to try to fix it, either by supporting a political party in an attempt to be heard, or running for office yourself. While there's good reason to be skeptical of anyone's ability to change the course of the major parties, there may be value in becoming engaged in the political process. Consider supporting a third party: There is no reason the United States is limited to two parties (most European countries have multiple parties), and the smaller parties could use help to build their prominence and support to overcome the barriers put in place by the Republicans and Democrats. And if you're interested in running for office, understand that you'll have the greatest chance for success—and for impact—by working at the local level, looking for a city council seat rather than a House seat or governorship.

KNOW THE LAW

As seen above, the government is keen on limiting your rights, and law enforcement officials won't hesitate to take advantage of your ignorance of the law if they can. So learn your rights: Understand what you're required to do at the orders of law enforcement, and what you can refuse to do. Take a look at resources such as those from the ACLU as an easy aid in protecting yourself.[219]

STAY WITHIN THE LAW

If you understand that people are trying to strip away your rights, there may be a temptation to rebel, to reclaim what you know is yours regardless of whether the current law allows it. This is a dangerous game to play: Whether you're right or not, and whether your conscience is clear or not, understand that the people with guns, who have the whole weight of the government behind them, will win whatever battle you think you're fighting. If you're going to fight, do so within the confines of the law. Be heard, but be safe.

CASE STUDY: THE AMERICAN COMMUNITY SURVEY

Most of us are familiar with the census that takes place every ten years in this country. It's one of the first activities mandated by the U.S. Constitution (appearing in Article I, Section 2), intended to generate a basic count of citizens by state so the federal government can determine the number of representatives and allocation of direct taxes.[220]

As you might expect from the U.S. government, however, politicians and bureaucrats decided they wanted more and more information over time, and so they began adding questions to this simple survey. They started adding questions with the 1940 census, and by the time the year 2000 rolled around, they found that the number of additional questions had become so burdensome that they had to break them out into a separate, standalone survey: The American Community Survey.

This survey, conducted annually with a random sampling of over 3 million U.S. households, represents a terrific level of government overreach. Some of the questions from the 2016 survey include:[221]

Questions about your residence

6   a.   How many separate rooms are in this house, apartment, or mobile home?

     b.   How many of these rooms are bedrooms?

7.   Does this house, apartment, or mobile home have—

     a.   hot and cold running water

     b.   a bathtub or shower?

     c.   a sink with a faucet?

     d.   a stove or range?

     e.   a refrigerator?

     f.   telephone service from which you can both make and receive calls? Include cell phones.

11. How many automobiles, vans, and trucks of one-ton capacity or less are kept at home for use by members of this household?

13. a.   LAST MONTH, what was the cost of electricity for this house, apartment, or mobile home?

     b.   LAST MONTH, what was the cost of gas for this house, apartment, or mobile home?

     c.   IN THE PAST 12 MONTHS, what was the cost of water and sewer for this house, apartment, or mobile home?

     d.   IN THE PAST 12 MONTHS, what was the cost of oil, coal, kerosene, wood, etc., for this house, apartment, or mobile home?

21. a.   Do you or any member of this household have a mortgage, deed of trust, contract to purchase, or similar debt on THIS property?

     b.   How much is the regular monthly mortgage payment on THIS property?

c. Does the regular monthly mortgage payment include payments for real estate taxes on THIS property?

d. Does the regular monthly mortgage payment include payments for fire, hazard, or flood insurance on THIS property?

Questions about you (for each person in your household):

16. Is this person CURRENTLY covered by any of the following types of health insurance or health coverage plans?

a. Insurance through a current or former employer or union (of this person or another family member)

b. Insurance purchased directly from an insurance company (by this person or another family member)

c. Medicare, for people 65 and older, or people with certain disabilities

d. Medicaid, Medical Assistance, or any kind of government-assistance plan for those with low incomes or a disability

e. TRICARE or other military health care

f. VA (including those who have ever used or enrolled for VA health care)

g. Indian Health Service

h. Any other type of health insurance or health coverage plan— Specify

31. How did this person usually get to work LAST WEEK?

32. How many people, including this person, usually rode to work in the car, truck, or van LAST WEEK?

33. What time did this person usually leave home to go to work LAST WEEK?

34. How many minutes did it usually take this person to get from home to work LAST WEEK?

47 INCOME IN THE PAST 12 MONTHS

a. Wages, salary, commissions, bonuses, or tips from all jobs.

b. Self-employment income from own nonfarm businesses or farm businesses, including proprietorships and partnerships.

c. Interest, dividends, net rental income, royalty income, or income from estates and trusts.

d. Social Security or Railroad Retirement

e. Supplemental Security Income (SSI)

f. Any public assistance or welfare payments from the state or local welfare office.

g. Retirement, survivor, or disability pensions

h. Any other sources of income received regularly such as Veterans' (VA) payments, unemployment compensation, child support or alimony.

The survey is well over twenty pages (it varies by year), and the government tells recipients that they are required to participate: Those who do not complete the survey are harassed repeatedly, first by phone and then by in-person visits (search "American Community Survey" on YouTube for examples), and they threaten people with fines of up to $5,000 for not complying.[222] Despite all the threats and harassment, however, no one has actually been prosecuted for noncompliance since 1970.[223]

Given how hard they push to make people answer their invasive questions, you might wonder what they do with the resulting data. While the government promotes the fact that it helps federal and state agencies make better decisions about their programs, they tend to downplay the fact that some of the biggest beneficiaries are businesses, using this free data to make better decisions on how and what to sell to you. Target brags openly about using survey data when deciding where to place stores and what to stock,[224] and when

Republicans threatened the program, a consortium of big business groups, including the National Association of Realtors, the National Association of Home Builders, the International Council of Shopping Centers, the National Restaurant Association, and the National Automobile Dealers Association, wrote to tell them how important this data was to them.[225]

So in essence, we have taxpayers paying for a program that requires them—under threat of harassment and fines—to answer deeply personal and private questions, all so businesses can get free data that helps them sell more. When the Founding Fathers introduced the idea of a population census, this is certainly not what they had in mind.

PART III

BIG BUSINESS

11

How you got screwed by . . .
BIG BUSINESS

In corporate culture, in sports culture, in the media, we honor
those who win at all costs.

—Jackson Katz

THE POINT:

There's nothing wrong with capitalism. But when big business uses
its money and political power to twist the rules in their favor—and
they do—we all suffer.

I have nothing against capitalism: In fact, as a small business
owner most of my life, I think it's a pretty great system. But it
only works if there's a level playing field.

And I think big businesses are fine, if they're big for the right
reasons. A big business is supposed to be big because they make a
great product, not because they're using their size and power to
cheat. And that's happening quite a bit these days.

Think back to the chapter on the big banks, and how their
size (remember "too big to jail"?) allowed them to commit crime
after crime and get away with small fines—and no prosecution at
all—each time they were caught. Or think about how the rich

and powerful—a group that includes many of today's big businesses—work to control how politicians vote.

These are just a couple of examples of how big business takes advantage of its size to change the rules, hurting its smaller competitors in the process. A few more examples follow.

LOBBYING

If your business can be affected by the rules created by politicians and government agencies, and if you have deep enough pockets, you can try to write or change those rules in your favor. And lobbying—defined as an attempt to influence legislation—has become big business, with $3.2 billion spent on this activity in 2015 alone (up from $1.4 billion in 1998).[226]

Which industries most want to influence legislation? In 2015, they included:[227]

- Medical Industries: $646 million
  (Includes pharmaceuticals/health products, insurance, hospitals/nursing homes, health professionals, and health services/HMOs)
- Energy: $247 million
  (Includes oil & gas, electric utilities)
- Finance: $163 million
  (Includes securities and investment, commercial banks)
- Tech Firms: $213 million
  (Includes electronics manufacturing and equipment, telecom services)

And others, including business associations ($128 million), defense firms ($74 million), civil servants and public officials

($71 million), and more. And what do these industries hope to accomplish by lobbying?

- They cut their own taxes by changing the law to carve out tax breaks. The Center for American Progress (CAP) notes that increasing lobbying by 1 percent is expected to reduce a corporation's tax rate between 0.5 percent and 1.6 percent, and that a $1 investment in lobbying is worth $6.65 in lower state corporate taxes.[228]
- They increase sales by inserting language that makes it easy for them to get contracts. CAP found that federal contracts were more likely to be awarded to firms that were active in lobbying.
- They craft laws that increase the size of their markets. The most obvious example is the Affordable Care Act, which was crafted in part by lobbyists for the medical and insurance industries, protecting their profitability and guaranteeing that millions of additional people would need to buy insurance.[229]

Corporate giving in politics has ramped up dramatically in recent years thanks to the 2010 *Citizens United* ruling by the Supreme Court. This ruling stated that freedom of speech applies to nonprofits, corporations, labor unions, and other associations, and that they cannot be prevented from donating to political causes. As a result, giving to Political Action Committees (PACs) exploded: According to the Campaign Finance Institute, total spending by PACs on House and Senate campaigns in 2008 (before the ruling) was $48.7 million; in 2016 it was $646.5 million.[230]

In addition to lobbying and providing campaign contributions, big business has one other trick up its sleeve: To influence politicians and government bureaucrats with the promise of big money when they leave public service. Remember Attorney General Eric Holder, who said that big banks were too big to prosecute? When he left office in 2015, he returned to his old legal practice, which defends clients including Morgan Stanley, Wells Fargo, Chase, Bank of America, and Citigroup—the same banks he refused to go after when he was in office.[231]

DECEIVING THE PUBLIC

Of course, lobbying—directly trying to influence legislation—is just a small part of big business's attempt to change the rules in their favor. They spend a lot more money trying to influence the public directly. The Center for Public Integrity offers the American Petroleum Institute as one example, noting that "the oil and gas industry trade group spent more than $7 million lobbying federal officials in 2012. But that sum was dwarfed by the $85.5 million it paid to four public relations and advertising firms to, in effect, lobby the American public . . ."[232]

How do they do it? A few techniques, pulled in part from the *Guardian* newspaper:[233]

- Frame indefensible positions as a "debate."
- Frame this debate by highlighting issues favorable to them and downplaying issues that are unfavorable.
- Leverage the media by granting reporters with access to important people, providing press backgrounders, and even writing articles for them.
- Conduct biased surveys that produce the results they want and then publicize those results.

- Create fake third-party "independent" groups that advocate for a position, also known as "astroturf" grassroots organizations.
- Sponsor scientific research and studies, which only get published if favorable to the industry.
- Sponsor a think tank to write and publish position papers favorable to an industry.
- Monitor and marginalize opposition groups, making it harder for them to gain attention and funding.
- Control the web, including editing Wikipedia pages, hosting Facebook pages, and publishing tweets from fake accounts and organizations, and posting favorable comments, and battling critics, on relevant websites.

Sharyl Attkisson, noted investigative journalist, gave a TED talk recently in which she explained how "astroturfing" works.[234] Paraphrasing her talk, suppose you hear about an effective new cholesterol drug that doctors should be prescribing, and wonder if it's too good to be true. You do a Google search, consult Facebook and Twitter, look at Wikipedia and WebMD, and you read the original study (from a peer-reviewed medical journal) behind the news report you saw. You see some naysayers online, but most people call them "quacks" and "nuts." And you find out that your own doctor just attended a medical seminar where they talked about how effective the drug is. But in reality, everything you had found in your research was false, planted there by PR firms and pharmaceutical companies.

UNFAIR PRACTICES

Thanks to their political connections and economic power, big business can get away with practices that are unfair, unethical, and/or work against the public good. A few examples:

Suppose you wanted a product that costs 10, 20, or 50 times more in the U.S. than in another country. It makes sense to buy it overseas, right? It does—and prescribed drugs have some of the greatest price disparities around. There are countless examples of drugs that cost more in the U.S. than elsewhere: As an extreme example, consider Sovaldi, a drug for hepatitis C, that costs $84,000 for a 12-week treatment in the U.S. but just $900 overseas.[235] But you can't legally get the overseas option. That's because, thanks to heavy lobbying by the drug companies, the Food and Drug Administration has made it illegal to import prescription drugs.

The Supplemental Nutrition Assistance Program (SNAP) was created so people in need could buy food. Given the size of the program, however—$74 billion serving 45+ million people in 2015[236]—you would expect big business to chase after that money. Which is why SNAP funds can now be used in some states to buy fast food like Taco Bell and KFC[237] as well as most kinds of junk food, including drinks like Red Bull, candy, and mixes for alcoholic beverages.[238] Lobbying wins again.

Every business wants to lower the costs of the things it buys. But big businesses take unfair advantage of their size to put a real squeeze on their vendors. Walmart, for example, is legendary here, forcing vendors to charge less and less and then taking longer and longer to pay them. As a result, those suppliers have to send jobs overseas, hurting the U.S. economy, and in fact several have been forced out of business by these practices.[239] And on top of that, the company forces small retailers out of business when it enters each new market, destroying local economies.[240]

CHEAP LABOR

In business, labor—the cost of paying people—is usually your single biggest expense. In order to boost profits, big business pushes for policies that benefit their bottom lines but hurt the rest of us.

Big business has been aggressively sending high-paying jobs overseas. According to the *Wall Street Journal*, "U.S. multinational corporations, the big brand-name companies that employ a fifth of all American workers . . . cut their work forces in the U.S. by 2.9 million during the 2000s while increasing employment overseas by 2.4 million, new data from the U.S. Commerce Department show."[241] IBM, for example, now employs more people in India than in the U.S., mostly because the average pay for a high-tech worker there is around $17,000 versus $100,000 here in the states.[242]

Big companies are largely in favor of immigration reform and amnesty.[243] The reason? It lowers their labor costs, which also then hurts U.S. citizens looking for jobs and decent wages. In the low-skilled market, the percentage of Americans without a high school degree who were employed fell from 54 percent in 2000 to 43 percent in 2009. Hourly wages for that group dropped by 22 percent between 1979 and 2007.[244] Those in the skilled trades fared no better: In an analysis of the construction industry in the Washington, DC area, researchers found that removing immigrant skilled labor from the market would result in an increase in the cost of trade labor by almost 70 percent.[245]

Another way that companies use cheap labor from overseas is the H1B program, which allows skilled workers from other countries to come to the U.S. to do jobs that could not otherwise be filled. That's the theory, at least: The reality is that they're often competing with local skilled workers and undercutting them on price. Consider Disney as one example, which hired 250 IT workers from India to replace their U.S. counterparts in 2015. The *New York Times* quotes one of those workers:

> "I just couldn't believe they could fly people in to sit at our desks and take over our jobs exactly," said one former worker, an American in his 40s who remains unemployed since his last day at Disney on Jan. 30. "It was so humiliating to train somebody else to take over your job. I still can't grasp it."[246]

ENVIRONMENTAL ARBITRAGE

"Arbitrage" simply means taking advantage of differences in the price of something; for example, wage arbitrage involves finding people in another country who will work for less than U.S. workers, which allows you to keep more of your profits for yourself, as noted in the previous section.

U.S. companies do the same thing for environmental protection laws: If the U.S. has very strict laws, and another country doesn't, companies will typically produce their goods in those less-restrictive countries in order to save money. China is just one example of a country that has allowed environmental destruction as it takes on manufacturing work from foreign companies. How bad is it?

Thanks to the lack of environmental controls in manufacturing and power generation, 460 million people in China are impacted by poor quality air, including 200 million who live in "hazardous" conditions defined as ten times the pollution levels set by the World Health Organization.[247] According to a newly released paper, outdoor air pollution contributes to the deaths of 4,400 people each day—a total of 1.6 million per year.[248]

The Council on Foreign Relations (CFR) notes that China has 20 percent of the world's population but only 7 percent of the world's fresh water supply. They say that "Industry along China's major water sources has polluted water supplies: In 2014, ground-water supplies in more than 60 percent of major cities were categorized as 'bad to very bad' and more than a quarter of China's key rivers are 'unfit for human contact.'"[249]

CFR also notes that more than 1 million square miles of China are turning into deserts due to pollution and poor farming practices;[250] other reports note that 20 percent of China's soil is contaminated, including some that are contaminated with heavy metals from factories.[251]

According to the United Nations' Intergovernmental Panel on Climate Change, this pollution results from rich countries outsourcing production of everything from clothes to smart phones.[252] In terms of clothing, Greenpeace names firms such as Adidas, Nike, Puma, Calvin Klein, Lacoste, and Abercrombie and Fitch for using "Chinese suppliers that pollute rivers with toxic, hormone-disrupting chemicals banned in Europe and elsewhere."[253] And the *Washington Post* details the effects on Chinese villages of mining graphite, a primary component in the lithium-ion batteries that power smart phones and other devices:[254]

By daylight, the particles are visible as a lustrous gray dust that settles on everything. It stunts the crops it blankets, begrimes laundry hung outside to dry and leaves grit on food. The village's well water has become undrinkable, too.

Beside the family home is a plot that once grew saplings, but the trees died once the factory began operating, said Zhang's husband, Yu Yuan.

"This is what we live with," Zhang said, slowly waving an arm at the stumps.

This environmental arbitrage allows companies to meet strict U.S. environmental guidelines—but the pollution doesn't go away, we're just shipping it overseas so the companies can save money and boost their profits. And millions of Chinese citizens suffer as a result.

Again, there's nothing wrong with being a big business, as long as you're playing by the rules—but as these many examples show, big businesses in the U.S. are bending or breaking the rules so that they benefit while the rest of us suffer.

CASE STUDY: THE FOOD PYRAMID

Because the government wields so much power and influence, anything it attempts becomes hopelessly mired in political lobbying, with companies attempting to shape and redirect it for their own interests. One case in point: The Food Pyramid.

From 1956 to 1992, the U.S. Department of Agriculture promoted healthy eating with its "Basic Four Food Groups" campaign, which encouraged people to include vegetables and fruits, meat, milk, and cereals and breads in their diets without suggesting a particular proportion.[255] That changed in 1992 when, modeling off a food pyramid campaign started in 1970 in Sweden, the U.S. government launched its own Food Pyramid.[256]

As you would expect, the USDA brought in a group of the nation's best nutritionists to design the pyramid and decide what portions of each type of food group were nutritionally appropriate. They submitted their findings and recommendations—and that's when the food industry swooped in. What happened next, according to Luise Light, Ed.D, the head of the panel:[257]

> Where we, the USDA nutritionists, called for a base of 5–9 servings of fresh fruits and vegetables a day, it was replaced with a paltry 2–3 servings (changed to 5–7 servings a couple of years later because an anti-cancer campaign by another government agency, the National Cancer Institute, forced the USDA to adopt the higher standard). Our recommendation of 3–4 daily servings of whole-grain breads and cereals was changed to a whopping 6–11 servings forming the base of the Food Pyramid as a concession to the processed wheat and corn industries. Moreover, my nutritionist group had placed baked goods made with white flour—including crackers, sweets and other low-nutrient foods laden with sugars and fats—at the peak of the pyramid, recommending that they be eaten sparingly. To our alarm, in the "revised" Food Guide, they were now made part of the Pyramid's base. And, in yet one more assault on dietary logic, changes were made to the wording of the dietary guidelines from "eat less" to "avoid too much," giving a nod to the processed-food industry interests by not limiting highly profitable "fun foods" (junk foods by any other name) that might affect the bottom line of food companies.

And, just to show that nothing ever really changes in Washington, DC, the exact same charges were leveled when the USDA revisited and revised the pyramid in 2015. As Dr. Walter Willett, chair of the Department of Nutrition at Harvard School of Public Health, noted, "The USDA's primary stakeholders are major food producers and manufacturers."[258]

Has the Food Pyramid helped with the country's obesity problem? Hardly: According to a CDC report, the obesity rate for adults age 20+ increased from 23 percent in an analysis between 1988–1994 to 34 percent in 2007–2008.[259] This doesn't prove that the Food Pyramid was the cause: The trend had already started around 1980, and other factors, such as increased portion sizes and sedentary lifestyles, played a role as well. But clearly the Food Pyramid did nothing to correct a very serious and growing problem.

12

How you got screwed by . . .
THE HEALTHCARE SYSTEM

I got the bill for my surgery. Now I know what those doctors were wearing masks for.

—James H. Boren

THE POINT:

Heath care costs are out of control, making billions for insurance companies, hospitals, and drug companies, while putting millions of Americans into bankruptcy or financial distress.

In a capitalist economy, innovation is supposed to force costs down and make products and services better over time. But when it comes to healthcare, the exact opposite has happened:

- As of 2014, the U.S. is spending more on healthcare as a percentage of GDP than any other country in the world. We spend 17.4 percent of GDP on healthcare (one-sixth of our total economy!) versus an international average of 8.8 percent.[260]
- Sure, there have been innovations in treatments. But can you say we offer better service when medical

errors are the third leading cause of death?[261] Or when we boast the highest chance of developed nations that a child will die before the age of five, the highest rate of women dying due to complications of pregnancy and childbirth, and the second highest rate of death by either coronary heart disease or lung disease?[262]

We're spending twice as much as the rest of the world for healthcare with middling-at-best results, and as a result we're driving people into poverty: Bankruptcies resulting from unpaid medical bills affected nearly 2 million people in 2013, and an additional 56 million people struggled with their medical bills.[263]

So what's going on? How can we have such an outrageously expensive system that produces such awful results?

WHAT "HEALTHCARE" COSTS

First, it will be helpful to get a handle on just how much we spend on healthcare, and how much healthcare spending has increased. On a per-person basis, spending has absolutely exploded; over the past thirty-five years, according to the Centers for Medicare and Medicaid, costs have increased in key categories as shown below (numbers are not adjusted for inflation):

Item	1980	1990	2000	2015
National Health Expenditures (total, all services)	$1,108	$2,843	$4,857	$9,990
Hospital Care	436	987	1,474	3,229
Physician and Clinical Services	207	624	1,024	1,979
Prescription Drugs	52	159	429	1,011
Net Cost of Health Insurance	40	124	228	655

For many of these categories, that's a doubling of per-person costs since the start of the new century. And some individual examples are even more stark:

- The cost of childbirth has increased dramatically over a very short period, with the cost of a regular birth rising from $7,737 to $12,520 (a 62 percent increase) and the cost of a Cesarean birth rising from $10,953 to $16,673 (a 52 percent increase) in just six years, between 2004 and 2010.[264]

- According to the *Journal of the American Medical Association*, 59 percent of the U.S. population aged twenty or higher took prescription drugs in 2011–2012, compared with 51 percent between 1999–2000. This includes 15 percent of the population taking five or more in 2011–2012, versus 8 percent in 1999–2000.[265] And the price of those prescription drugs is skyrocketing, both for name-brand drugs like Pyrimethamine, which recently increase from $13.50 to $750 per tablet, and the Epipen, which increased in price by 500 percent,[266] as well as generic medicines like fentanyl citrate (a powerful painkiller), which increased from 50 cents to $37.49 per dose, or the asthma drug albuterol sulfate, which went up more than 3,400 percent.[267]

- The table above refers to the net cost of health insurance, which is what individuals pay in versus the benefits they receive. If you look at the total annual cost of insurance, it has nearly tripled: Since the year 2000, the total annual cost of an average family policy has increased from $6,772 to $17,322 in 2015.[268]

Going forward, according to the Centers for Medicare and Medicaid Services, the problem will only get worse. From 2015 to 2025, health spending is going to grow at a rate of 5.8 percent per year, which is 1.3 percent faster than gross domestic product (we'll leave aside here the unrealistic assumption that GDP will grow 4.5 percent per year). If these projections are correct, the health share of GDP is expected to rise from 17.5 percent in 2014 to 20.1 percent by 2025.[269]

How did things get so bad? There are several causes.

RISE OF THE MIDDLEMAN

If you can buy something direct from a manufacturer instead of a retailer, you expect that you'll save some money, right? The retailer has to mark up everything he or she sells, as does the distributor that moves the product between the two.

The same principle holds true in healthcare. Years ago, most people didn't have health insurance; they would just pay the doctor directly for routine visits and basic services. If something costly and expensive happened, many had catastrophic insurance which would cover emergency situations.

Today, however, we have allowed health insurance companies to insert themselves into most medical transactions, and the government (Medicare, Medicaid) to put itself in the middle of the rest.

That drives up costs a lot, not only because we have to pay all those insurance employees, but also because doctors' offices and hospitals have to similarly staff up to handle all the additional paperwork.

But more importantly, it means they can charge what they want since you, the customer, have no idea what you're being charged. How much did the doctor's office bill you for your last visit? You may know your co-pay amount, but we're talking about the actual cost of the visit. If you've been in the hospital, how much did they charge for the room, the food, or the pain medicine? Most people have no idea. And that lack of awareness makes it easy for them to jack up the prices.

ILLEGAL BILLING PRACTICES

Would you hire a service that refused to give you a price up front, and billed you whatever they wanted to after the fact? Especially if they could add on services when you weren't even able to approve them? That's what we're allowing hospitals and doctors to do whenever we sign off on anything more than a routine procedure. There are a handful of sites that will give you up-front pricing—see the Surgery Center of Oklahoma as an example[270]— but for the most part we're giving up all control over costs when we walk through the hospital doors. And the price swings can be unbelievable: When comparing emergency room bills from several hospitals, researchers found that the treatment price for a sprained ankle varied from $4 or up to $24,110![271]

Doctors and hospitals also use discriminatory pricing—in other words, they charge some people more than others for the exact same thing. A hospital may bill a certain procedure for $1,000; if you have insurance, the hospital may actually charge $600 due to discounts negotiated by the company, but if you don't have insurance—probably because you can't afford it in the first place—they'll bill you the full $1,000. The hospital overcharged just so they could get the payment they wanted for the service in the first place.[272]

What about extreme overcharging for routine supplies? How about $1.50 for a single acetaminophen pill, $283 for an X-ray when the hospital accepts $20.44 from Medicare, or $15,000 for multiple blood and lab tests when Medicare would have paid just a few hundred dollars in all?[273] Ridiculous overcharges seem to be the norm, as a way to make profits or cover the cost of those who can't or won't pay for service.

LACK OF COMPETITION

A lack of competition gives doctors, hospitals, and medical suppliers with even more pricing power, and it happens in a few ways:

- The medical field has substantially limited competition through its licensing policies. Of course we all want proof that doctors and other health care providers are qualified; but licensing is used to prevent providers of alternative therapies from practicing, and to prevent non-licensed people from providing more routine types of care.[274] In addition, licensing bodies strongly discourage members from competing on price, removing an important factor from patient decisions.[275]
- The healthcare field—including insurance companies, hospitals, and doctors—has developed "preferred provider" networks that are akin to vertical monopolies. These give each member of the network much higher levels of pricing power, driving costs up.[276]
- We've already talked about how the drug companies made it illegal to import their drugs from overseas, where they sell them at a much lower rate than in the U.S.. But to further reduce competition, they're also very involved in lobbying on patent laws. Patents

create short-term monopolies: When you have exclusive rights to sell an important drug, you can charge whatever the market will bear. And that makes sense for a time, given the costs to invent new drugs. But drug companies have found a way to unethically extend those patent protections, either by paying generic drug companies not to make copies after patents expire; forcing patients onto new drugs (with longer patent lives); or by tinkering with the formula in ways that don't really make a difference, yet allow them to apply for a new patent.[277] All of these strategies protect fat profits while hurting patients.

BALLOONING COSTS

The U.S. has a rapidly aging population and, as you might expect, the older people get, the more medical care they require: According to the Centers for Medicare and Medicaid Services, "Per person personal health care spending for the 65 and older population was $18,988 in 2012, over 5 times higher than spending per child ($3,552) and approximately 3 times the spending per working-age person ($6,632)."[278] As a result, while the population age 65+ was less than 14 percent in 2012, they accounted for 34 percent of all medical spending.[279] When you consider the demographic tidal wave that's beginning to hit with the retirement of the Baby Boomers, growing from 13 percent of the population to 21.7 percent between 2010 and 2040,[280] you can only imagine how medical spending is going to explode in this country.

WHEN ALL YOU HAVE IS A HAMMER . . .

When you have all kinds of advanced technology and science at hand, and you've invested years of your life in learning how to use them, your inclination will be to take advantage of those tools when treating patients.

For those who practice medicine, there is a real and demonstrated "intervention bias"—running tests, performing procedures, and prescribing pills even when it would be perfectly reasonable to take a wait-and-see approach, or pursue a much lighter touch. There are many reasons for this bias, including the financial interests of the medical provider, their need to feel that they're taking an active response, a fear of lawsuits, and even the patients' own demand for aggressive care.[281] Regardless of the reason, this bias results in much more medical intervention than may be warranted, often at great cost.

None of the practices listed here were done to benefit patients: They were all done to boost the profits and monopoly powers of the companies providing services. And those rapidly-rising costs will continue to go up unless this is somehow addressed.

13

How you got screwed by . . .
BIG MEDIA

I do not mean to imply that television news deliberately aims to deprive Americans of a coherent, contextual understanding of their world. I mean to say that when news is packaged as entertainment, that is the inevitable result. And in saying that the television news show entertains but does not inform, I am saying something far more serious than that we are being deprived of authentic information. I am saying we are losing our sense of what it means to be well informed.

—Neil Postman, *Amusing Ourselves to Death*

THE POINT:

The media is no longer a watchdog working on behalf of the public; it is owned by, and serves, those in power, and influences you in ways that serve their interests and their agenda.

When I graduated college, our keynote speaker was Ben Bradlee, who served as editor at the *Washington Post* during the Watergate scandal. He said something that shocked me: That "we (i.e., the media) decide what the truth is." What he meant by that was that if the newspapers and TV stations all ran a story, that's what people are going to believe, whether or not it is actually true. It was a frightening thought then, and it's a frightening thought now.

This matters quite a bit, because the media is no longer "The Fourth Estate," a phrase describing a time (very, very long ago) when the media served almost as a fourth branch of government, acting as a watchdog that kept other institutions honest and truly served the public through its relentless investigative efforts. Instead, the mass media is now almost wholly owned by big corporations and serves their interests, and not yours.

How big is Big Media? Today, just six corporations own more than 90 percent of the major media outlets (including TV, radio, and print media); compare that with the fact that in 1983, 90 percent of the media was owned by 50 companies.[282] As of 2015, Comcast Corporation is the largest media conglomerate in the U.S., with the Walt Disney Company, Twenty-First Century Fox, and Time Warner ranking second, third, and fourth respectively.[283]

The effects are clear: The media has turned into a corporate mouthpiece, saying whatever serves the interests of these big companies. Is it any wonder that the U.S. has dropped to 41st place in rankings of media freedom?[284] Or that, according to Gallup, in 2016 "Americans' trust and confidence in the mass media 'to report the news fully, accurately and fairly' has dropped to its lowest level in Gallup polling history, with 32 percent saying they have a great deal or fair amount of trust in the media"?[285]

THE PROFIT MOTIVE

One of the biggest issues is the corporate profit motive: When media cares more about the bottom line than about good reporting, they cut all kinds of corners.

This is most visible in the number of reporters on the job. The newspaper industry, for example, which is already seeing declines in readership as people go online, shed over twenty thousand jobs between 1994 and 2014—a 39 percent decline—as owners worked to maintain profitability.[286] Coverage was further damaged as most newspapers and broadcast outlets shuttered most or all of their foreign bureaus, resulting in far less coverage of crucial international news.[287]

How do they find content now? It's not through original reporting. Most newspapers and media outlets get their stories through licensing, resulting in identical content going out through multiple channels. They run press releases, often word for word. And they even use software to automatically write articles like corporate reports or sports stories. But what they're not doing is original reporting or critical thinking or analysis.

PROTECTING THEIR INTERESTS

What do you think would happen if you openly bad-mouthed your boss, calling out his or her flaws or mistakes to your co-workers and customers? You likely wouldn't last long with that company. For that exact same reason, members of the media will overlook negative coverage of the people who can get them fired or hurt their professional prospects, a group that includes their corporate owners, advertisers, regulators (i.e. the government), and the influential people they need access to for interviews and quotes.

As one example, the list of crimes committed by major banks and investment firms (detailed in Chapter 2) is jaw-dropping; how much coverage have you seen in the financial press, from CNBC or the *Wall Street Journal*? Aside from minimal reporting on specific news events, there's been a virtual media blackout in order to protect these lucrative advertisers and their access to powerful figures for information and interviews.

And sometimes the protection is subtler, such as in the recent case of a two-year-old being killed by an alligator at a Disney resort. While ABC (owned by Disney) did cover the story, they failed to bring up questions about Disney's responsibility to protect its guests with signs and other warnings, a topic that was covered extensively by the other major networks.[288]

As Chris Hedges, author and former reporter for the *New York Times*, said of that paper, "The rules aren't written on the walls, but everyone knows, even if they do not articulate it, the paper's unofficial motto: *Do not significantly alienate those upon whom we depend for money and access!*"[289]

MISDIRECTION

How many stories have you heard this week about celebrities? And how many have you heard about U.S. military interventions in countries like Yemen? When the media try to fill your head with the Kardashians, they're keeping serious issues out of consideration.

The same thing happens when serious newsmakers place themselves into less-than-serious media: President Obama had notably granted interviews to YouTube stars (right after the 2015 State of the Union address no less), appeared in the farcical "Between Two Ferns" interview series, and became a fixture on the late night show circuit. In doing so, he maintained his visibility without having to answer serious questions, leaving the public feeling that they have access without actually getting any real information.

KEEPING YOU AFRAID

How much do you see about terrorism in the news? Probably a lot: It has a constant presence in the media, with nonstop coverage whenever a terrorist event happens, and an ongoing focus in coverage otherwise.

But the tremendous amount of news coverage doesn't line up with the danger. For example, the CDC reports the top causes of death as follows (for 2014):[290]

Heart disease:	614,348
Cancer:	591,699
Chronic lower respiratory diseases:	147,101
Accidents (unintentional injuries):	136,053
Stroke (cerebrovascular diseases):	133,103
Alzheimer's disease:	93,541
Diabetes:	76,488
Influenza and pneumonia:	55,227
Nephritis, nephrotic syndrome, and nephrosis:	48,146
Intentional self-harm (suicide):	42,773

How many deaths from terrorism in 2014? None in the U.S., while 24 U.S. citizens were killed from terrorist acts overseas.[291] While every death from terrorism is a tragedy, it hardly compares with the 614,348 from heart disease.

And yet we have almost nonstop coverage and conversation around terrorism. The reason is clear: To keep you afraid, which allows those in power a tremendous opportunity to rule. It allows them to install and maintain the TSA (with its 95 percent failure rate); pass and reauthorize the ironically-named Patriot Act, which has done more to curtail our rights than any other piece of legislation;[292] and turbocharge intelligence gathering efforts on U.S. citizens like those uncovered by Edward Snowden.[293]

Benjamin Franklin famously stated, "Those who would give up essential liberty to purchase a little temporary safety, deserve neither liberty nor safety." He likely did not count on our own media to be the ones scaring us into compliance.

MEDIA BIAS

As noted previously, Gallup has found that just 32 percent of Americans trust the media to report the news fairly and accurately; those numbers differ based on people's political affiliations, with 51 percent of Democrats trusting the media versus 30 percent of independent voters and just 14 percent of Republicans.[294] The wide gap between people of different political leanings reinforces the common belief that this bias is liberal: We're much less likely to see bias when our views are shared by those in the news.

Some journalists point to the fact that most don't self-identify with a political party: In a 2014 study, 7 percent identified as Republican, 28 percent as Democrat, 50 percent as independent, and 15 percent as "other."[295] But if you look at the behavior of reporters themselves, their political leanings are clear: 88 percent of political donations from members of the media went to Obama and the Democrats in 2008,[296] donations by media firms tilted "heavily" to Obama in 2012,[297] and, in the 2016 campaign cycle, 96 percent of political donations from journalists went to Hillary Clinton's campaign.[298] (It's hard to analyze the voting records of journalists, since many choose not to vote in order to avoid a perceived conflict of interest, which apparently does not extend to their giving habits.)

How does this bias play out? A few examples:

It Depends . . .

Sometimes what the media covers, and what they say about it, depends on which political party is holding the reins of power. Consider the attitude of Paul Krugman, economic writer for the *New York Times*, towards deficits. When George W. Bush was president, deficits were terrible things, which would cause a "collapse of confidence some time in the not-too-distant future." Once Barack Obama was in office, however, running far larger deficits than Bush could have dreamed of, we suddenly had to guard against "deficit hysteria," even saying that deficits should be bigger.[299] Unbelievably, after Donald Trump won the White House, Krugman suddenly felt that "deficits matter again."[300]

What They Cover—or Not

In the most recent presidential race, both Hillary Clinton and Donald Trump had a fair amount of baggage, but the media decided to focus on one candidate's challenges without covering the other's. The Hill notes that Trump's controversial comments about women were emerging at the same time as the Podesta WikiLeaks emails about Clinton's campaign, but the press found only one of those scandals to be newsworthy. In one night, the ABC, NBC, and CBS nightly news shows offered more than 23 minutes of coverage of Trump's scandal, and spent just one minute and seven seconds on Clinton's issues. That same day, the *New York Times* ran eleven negative stories on Trump, and none on Clinton. ABC and the *Washington Post* did a voter survey shortly thereafter, and included six questions on Trump's treatment of women, and none on Clinton's WikiLeaks revelations.[301]

Pushing an Agenda

Most liberal journalists are in favor of unrestricted immigration, and that perspective is evident in their reporting. When they report on immigrants who came here illegally, the word "illegal" is never used; they're either "undocumented," simply identified as immigrants or not identified at all, especially in negative situations such as describing a crime suspect. Stories are often told from their perspective, and not from the perspective of those who they have affected, such as citizens who struggle to find work in a market where illegal immigrants compete for jobs and are willing to work for less. And reporters quote sources selectively, such as the *New York Times* reporter who argued for amnesty by citing a questionable study pointing to increased tax revenues for state and local agencies, while ignoring a consensus among economists that most immigrants would actually represent a drain on taxpayers.[302]

Using Polls to Shape the Narrative

Polls can be helpful in understanding an issue: People like hard numbers, and they can tell us how are fellow citizens feel about an issue. But they're also easy to rig in order to get the answers you want, and the media are experienced at manipulating them. One way to do this is to skew your sample: For example, in a recent poll from ABC and the *Washington Post*, 23 percent of their responses came from Republicans, even though 29 percent of the public identifies with that party.[303] They can also write the survey questions in a way that gives them the answers they want: In a previous poll during the primary season, these same people asked the question: If Trump and Clinton were joined by Mitt Romney running as an independent, which way would you vote? Of course, Romney had given no indication at all of running, but by splitting the Republican response they were able to show Clinton in the lead.[304]

Mark Twain said that "If you don't read the newspaper, you're uninformed. If you read the newspaper, you're mis-informed." What he didn't say was that the misinformation was by design, intended to protect the powers that be and advance an agenda.

14

CAVEAT EMPTOR: BIG BUSINESS

These are the rules of big business. They have superseded the teachings of our parents and are reducible to a simple maxim: Get a monopoly; let Society work for you; and remember that the best of all business is politics, for a legislative grant, franchise, subsidy or tax exemption is worth more than a Kimberly or Comstock lode, since it does not require any labor, either mental or physical, for its exploitation.

—Frederic Howe

Let's be honest: It's really hard to protect yourself as a consumer today. We have so many demands on our time and attention, and there are so many corporations trying to sell us so many products and services that it's almost impossible to make smart decisions.

Just walking into the grocery store can be overwhelming: According to the Food Marketing Institute, the number of products in an average grocery store grew from 8,948 to almost 47,000 between 1975 and 2008.[305] If you want to brush your teeth, you have to choose from upwards of 353 different types and sizes of toothpaste; if you want to wash your hair, there are 187 types of shampoo to consider.[306] Whether you're buying groceries, insurance, or a new phone, it's very difficult to fully explore your options and make sure you're not getting screwed by corporations that may be trying to overcharge you or take advantage of you in some way.

Not only do we have to navigate through an ocean of products and services, we have to worry about the companies behind them. Are they sending the work overseas, taking advantage of lower wages and relaxed environmental standards? Are they lobbying to create an unfair advantage over smaller competitors? Are they a company I can respect, or are they doing things in secret that hurt me and others?

If you have the time and the dedicated passion, you can invest the significant amount of time it would take to thoroughly research all of your purchasing decisions. But failing that—if you just don't have the time available to do that—here are several steps you can take to protect yourself.

BUY LOCAL

Wherever possible, buy from people in your community. Look for local farmers rather than buying fruits and vegetables at the grocery store, where they might come from major corporations and require shipping halfway around the world. Buy your cookies from a local baker rather than the preservative-filled treats found at the store. Bank with a community bank or credit union rather than the "too big to fail" bank. That keeps money in the community and gives you a much closer tie to the things you buy.

BUY FROM SMALL BUSINESSES

Go to the small "mom and pop" stores rather than the national chains: You'll probably find better products and services at comparable prices. If you're a coffee drinker, you'll probably enjoy a homegrown coffee shop much more than one of the national brands. The locally-owned bike store will have better products and service than a nationally-known retailer. Buying from your neighbors keeps the local economy strong and ensures your money won't be used in ways you don't approve.

BUY SIMPLE

One of the ways big corporations take advantage of people is to make things as complicated as possible: This is especially true in areas like technology and financial services. By keeping things simple, you'll make it easier to assess what you're getting without lots of confusing elements thrown in to the mix to distract you. Michael Pollan suggests the "five ingredient rule" for foods[307]— i.e., don't eat anything with more than five ingredients in it. Carry that same simple and clean philosophy forward into all your purchases.

DO IT YOURSELF

The ultimate, and most empowering, way to avoid corporate trickery is to do things yourself. Start a garden and grow some of your own food. Bake your own bread, and cook your own meals. While this doesn't apply to every area—very few of us could build our own cars—it can certainly be applied in a few circumstances.

RELY ON WORD OF MOUTH

Most of us get our information on products and services from the companies themselves, through their advertising and information on their websites. But how much do you trust these companies to tell you the unvarnished truth? A better source is the word of other consumers, people who share their own experiences after buying something. There are lots of affinity and product review websites online that can help; however, since even these can be corrupted by corporate marketers (it's called "astro-turfing"—fake grassroots work), keep a critical eye out for fake reviews. The best source for recommendations is people you personally know, such as family, friends, and coworkers.

DECIDE ON YOUR OWN SIMPLE STANDARDS

There are so many issues that could concern people about corporate activity. Are they using genetically modified ingredients? Are they taking advantage of relaxed standards overseas? Are they anticompetitive? And different companies may be crossing the line in some areas and not others. To keep things simple, decide on the issues most important to you and use those as your standard as a consumer. While it would be ideal to be able to do a "deep dive" on every single corporation you buy from, it's more realistic to work through a filter of essential items to avoid getting overwhelmed.

SEND A MESSAGE

Remember that the only reason big corporations have power is that lots of people are buying their products: Without sales, they wouldn't have the money and profits to do what they do. If you have a problem with a corporation, vote with your feet: Refuse to buy what they sell. If a bank like Wells Fargo creates millions of secret accounts in their customers' names, their customers send them a message by either moving their accounts or staying. Customers who stay tell them that their behavior is all right; those who leave show that it's not.

CASE STUDY: ETHANOL

Ethanol, which is essentially grain alcohol made from organic materi-
als like corn and used as a gasoline alternative, is not new: Invented
in 1826, it was used in Henry Ford's Model T, and relied on heavily
during World War II due to fuel shortages. Given its history, it's
understandable that people turned again to ethanol in the 1970s
when they became concerned about the environmental impact of oil
drilling and use, and when the availability of gasoline again became
an issue.[308]

But we know a lot more about ethanol than we did in 1826. For
example:

- Ethanol produces 35 percent less energy than gasoline, meaning
  it's less efficient. *Consumer Reports* tested a Chevrolet Tahoe
  with regular gasoline and then with an 85 percent gasoline/15
  percent ethanol mix, and saw fuel economy in highway driving
  drop from 21 miles per gallon to 15.[309]
- Ethanol harms your engine. People have long known that ethanol
  damages small engines, like those in lawnmowers, causing metal
  parts to corrode and plastic and rubber parts to degrade, leading to
  harder starts and shorter engine life.[310] And the damaging effects
  are greater as you increase the amount of ethanol in the mix: In
  fact, most car makers have stated that they will void warranties on
  cars found to be using fuel with 15 percent or more ethanol.[311]
- Ethanol has damaging environmental and economic effects. In
  the 1970s, people assumed that ethanol was better for the environment since it didn't involve drilling. And while it does reduce
  overall output of carbon dioxide, further study has shown that it
  increases the output of other volatile compounds, and the growing

and processing of corn uses additional energy that produces its own impact. Further, diverting corn crops into ethanol increases the cost of corn-based foods and those that rely on corn as feed, which has a particularly large impact on the poor.[312]

Yet despite all of this, ethanol production has skyrocketed. According to *Forbes*, "In 2000, over 90 percent of the U.S. corn crop went to feed people and livestock, many in undeveloped countries, with less than 5 percent used to produce ethanol. In 2013, however, 40 percent went to produce ethanol, 45 percent was used to feed livestock, and only 15 percent was used for food and beverage."[313]

If you want to know why, look no further than Washington, DC. In 2005, Congress passed the Energy Policy Act, which requires gasoline to contain 10 percent ethanol through a renewable fuel standard program. The EPA subsequently established regulations allowing for the sale of 15 percent ethanol gas for cars that can accommodate it.

And why would they do this? One word: Iowa.

In presidential politics, Iowa is a critically important state: It's one of the first in the country to hold caucus every four years, so a win here, or even a good showing, is necessary to establish a politician. And to win in Iowa, you need the support of corn producers—which means supporting ethanol, which politicians have done through tax breaks, tariffs on foreign competitors, and then finally federal mandates.[314]

While the ethanol lobby's power seems to be on the decline—Ted Cruz won the Republican primary there despite his opposition to the renewable fuel standard program—it will take time to reverse the effects of lobbyists' and politicians' collaboration against the interests of consumers.

PART IV

TAKING ACTION

15

ROOT ELEMENTS OF A SCREW JOB

If you've been playing poker for half an hour and you still
don't know who the patsy is, you're the patsy.

—Warren Buffett

THE POINT:

If you can identify some of the common elements of a screw job, you
can avoid situations in the future in which you might get screwed.

If you've read through the book to this point, the topics and
examples have probably started to feel familiar, as if they all have
some things in common. And in fact, there are some strong
themes running through them; if you can learn to recognize
those commonalities, you may be able to avoid being taken
advantage of the next time someone wants to screw you. What
are those common elements?

OTHER PEOPLE'S MONEY

Many people consider John F. Kennedy one of our greatest presidents, but he is also responsible for a world-class mistake: On

January 17, 1962, he signed Executive Order 10988, which recognized the right for federal employees to collectively bargain. Why would this be a mistake? Because when government workers negotiate with politicians, there is no counterparty: No one is representing the people who provide the dollars. Politicians don't: they want the support of unions, and are happy to promise taxpayer dollars in return. As a result, government employees have benefited greatly, and today the average government worker earns 80 percent more than his private sector counterpart when benefits are included in the calculation.[315]

We tend to be very careful when spending our own money, but when someone else spends on our behalf—especially if they "represent" us but we don't actually know them—it's unlikely that our interests are their main motivation. Politicians love to spend our money "for the common good," but if you think about the massive numbers of silly or ill-thought-out projects and incredible amount of waste, it's crystal clear that our interests are the last thing on their minds.

MORE COMPLICATED THAN IT SHOULD BE

The Gettysburg Address has 272 words. The Declaration of Independence has 1,337. The Affordable Care Act has 381,517 words contained within 2,700 pages, and as of 2013 there were already an additional 11,588,500 words of associated regulations.[316] How could anyone read that to know what's in it, and whether or not they're in compliance? Even members of the Supreme Court admitted that they weren't able to read the whole thing when they were ruling on its Constitutionality; Justice Scalia said that forcing him to read it may violate the Eighth Amendment, the one that prohibits cruel and unusual punishment.[317]

When things are more complicated than they need to be, or

should be, there's an opportunity to insert things that can be used to take advantage of others. Whether it's a law, a financial agreement, or a clause you skip over as you agree to the terms of a software license, excessive complication is a warning sign that someone might be trying to hide something that's not in your interest.

NO WATCHDOG

Our system of government was designed to have checks and balances, to prevent people from gaining too much power and acting without any restraint. In the same way, we set up regulators to watch big business and prevent them from acting unethically or illegally.

Both of those systems are broken. Presidents of both parties have pushed the limits of their authority without any resistance from Congress. Remember, for example, that the Constitution says that only Congress can issue a declaration of war, and the last time they did that was in 1942 when we declared war on Bulgaria, Hungary, and Romania as part of our efforts in World War II.[318] Since that time, Congress has instead issued resolutions that give the President wide military discretion, such as the Gulf of Tonkin Resolution that opened the door to Vietnam, or the Authorization for the use of Military Force that was passed in the aftermath of the September 11 terrorist attacks to target the Taliban in Afghanistan, and which has since been used by presidents Bush and Obama to justify thirty-seven different acts of war in countries including Djibouti, Yemen, Kenya, Syria, Libya, and many others in circumstances where Congress never issued a declaration of war.

On the regulatory front, our system is utterly broken: There is a revolving door between industries and their regulatory agencies, with former bankers found in leadership and staff positions within the Securities and Exchange Commission, Treasury Department, Department of Justice, Office of the Comptroller of the Currency, and Office of Management and Budget during President Obama's tenure,[319] and President Trump having already nominated several alumnae of Goldman Sachs to senior positions.[320] Similar career moves happen in almost every regulated industry, resulting in government officials who have a bias towards the industries in which they used to work, and a need to "play nice" in order to ensure future job opportunities. There is simply no way for us to trust our leadership and regulators if they have such blatant conflicts of interest.

NO CONSEQUENCES

Before the 2008 financial crisis, there was the Savings and Loan Crisis in the 1980s, which saw widespread fraud as bankers tried to prevent the public from becoming aware that their institutions were bankrupt. As a result, according to Bill Black, one of the prosecutors involved, "the savings and loan regulators made over thirty thousand criminal referrals, and this produced over one thousand felony convictions in cases designated as 'major' by the Department of Justice." They ended up with a 90 percent conviction rate, almost unheard of when it comes to white-collar crimes.[321]

Given that the 2008 financial crisis was seventy times as large as the S&L Crisis, both in terms of losses and the amount of fraud,[322] one would expect a similar increase in referrals and convictions. Yet, as of April 2016, just thirty-five bankers had been sentenced to prison, all of them from banks with $10 billion or less in assets.[323] No one from one of Attorney General Eric Holder's "too big to jail" banks had been accused of any crimes;

they all walked away scot-free, simply by returning a small portion of their profits as penalties for their actions without admitting any guilt.

There are two things that prevent people from committing crimes: Ethics and a fear of punishment. When the fear of punishment is gone, people without ethics have no reason to play by the rules, which means that you, and everyone else, are in danger from these predators.

REFUSING TO ACKNOWLEDGE THE LIMITS ON GROWTH

When you think about it, most of our lives—both individually and as a country—are based on the idea of growth. We want our incomes and retirement accounts to grow. Our businesses are supposed to increase sales every year. We keep a close eye on the growth in GDP as a barometer on our country's health. But in just about every case, there are limits as to how much you can grow.

It would be nice to think that we accepted these limits; unfortunately, the truth is that when we hit our limits, some of us start looking for ways to push through them, often in ways that have severe consequences in the long term. When farmers hit a limit in crop growth, they might turn to genetically modified seeds. When we hit a limit in oil production, we start fracking, which involves pumping millions of gallons of toxic chemicals into the earth to force out the last remaining oil.

"Growth is good" has become a national mantra, one that causes all sorts of problems in its refusal to acknowledge the limits in every system.

SHORT-TERM THINKING

In all too many cases, we have decided to trade immediate gain for long-term pain. Consider how we treat money as an example. What happens when we earn as much as we can, but we still want more? The answer used to be sacrifice: If we didn't have it, we did without. The answer today, however, is that we'll spend what we don't have without even a second thought, thanks to borrowing and credit. And that goes for people, businesses, and governments, which is how we've amassed more than $63 trillion in debt as a country[324]—an amount that can never be paid back.

The same principle applies to many of our corporate and government benefit programs, such as pension plans, Social Security, and Medicare. The people who put these plans into place reap tremendous rewards in terms of employee and public goodwill, and will almost certainly not be around to deal with promises that will be impossible to fulfill in the future. Beware those arrangements that sound as if they're too good to be true, because in the long run most of them are.

16

THE END GAME

Stocks have reached what looks like a permanently high plateau.
—Economist Irving Fisher, three days before the stock
market crash that triggered the Great Depression

THE POINT:

No one knows for sure what the end game looks like, or when it happens. But it won't be too long, and it won't be a happy ending.

Let's be clear: I don't know how things are going to play out in the future, nor do I know when we'll hit any sort of a breaking point that would welcome in a crisis. (No one else does, either, so be cautious of people who say they know what's going to happen in the coming months or years.)

But I do know that we're not on a sustainable path. All of the problems described in this book are growing and build on one another to create a sort of "pressure cooker" environment that cannot go on forever. Just think about how the trends we see today feed off each other to create the ideal conditions for some sort of economic or social disruption:

- Despite the government's claims of low inflation, the

price to consumers of most things—including but not limited to food, housing, medical care, and education—continue to rise.

- Debts of all kinds—personal, corporate, and government—are rapidly increasing. The federal government's debt is sitting at the $20 trillion mark, making America the greatest debtor in the history of the world.
- After a 35-year decline in interest rates, allowing more and more borrowing, we have bottomed out and started to move back up, making borrowing more expensive and threatening the longest-running bond bull market in history.
- Wages have not risen in real terms since 1979.[325]
- We have a huge percentage of the population moving into retirement age, where they will stop contributing to the tax base, start requiring more government services, and depress asset prices as they sell their investments.
- Income inequality is at the highest level since the Great Depression,[326] and movements such as Occupy Wall Street show an increased awareness—and resentment—of that fact.
- Our social tapestry is fraying, with trust in various institutions at or near record lows[327] and disruptive domestic movements ranging from the Tea Party to Black Lives Matter.

The economist Herbert Stein offered Stein's Law, which said that "If something cannot go on forever, it will stop."[328] With that truth in mind, think about whether any or all of the trends above can go on forever. How long can prices continue to increase while wages remain stagnant? Can debts continue to rise forever as interest rates climb? What will happen to the federal deficit as interest rates go up?

And what happens as some of these trends reverse? If the government cannot keep on borrowing $1 trillion per year, what happens to the wave of retirees who need Social Security, Medicare, and other government services? If wages continue to stagnate, how long before peoples' resentment of record income inequality leads to an active response?

WHAT WOULD A DISRUPTION LOOK LIKE?

As I said, I don't know what will happen: There are a lot of very smart people who differ on even fundamental questions, like whether these factors are more likely to lead to inflation (or even hyperinflation) or deflation. A lot of it depends on what some powerful players, like the government and Federal Reserve, do in response to early crises, and there's no way to predict with certainty how they'll act.

But I'll go out on a limb and tell you what I think might happen.

For context, remember that in 2008, the Federal Reserve got caught flat-footed as people failed to make loan payments and the resulting defaults spread throughout the system, crushing both lenders and investors. The Fed poured a flood of liquidity into the system, removed many of the rules that were causing problems (such as "mark to market"), and directly bought up trillions of dollars of bad debts and other assets to create demand in a market that sorely needed it. Finally, to spur confidence, they directly intervened in the financial markets to levitate the price of assets, hoping to create a wealth effect that restored confidence and investment.

Rightly or wrongly, their response worked—but what was supposed to be a temporary fix turned into a permanent state of intervention. The markets knew that there was a Fed "put" and investors, mostly institutional investors, piled back into the market. The day was saved, at least for the time being. But the absence of any real reforms left a financial system that looked good on the surface but was continuing to rot on the inside.

Like the military, I think those in power tend to prepare for and fight the last war. And in this case, the Fed is ready to prevent widespread defaults by again pumping money into the system and further relaxing rules. A case in point is the fracking industry, which borrowed tremendous sums of money when oil prices were high, and found themselves in deep distress when the bottom fell out of the market: Banks significantly relaxed loan terms to allow firms to avoid defaulting,[329] and there are rumors that this was done at the insistence of the Federal Reserve.[330]

In the big picture, the fracking industry is small potatoes in terms of default amounts. What happens when a larger market hits a stress point? Suppose the housing market crashes again (keeping in mind that prices are higher than they were at the 2007 peak)? Suppose we acknowledge the nonpayment issue in the $1.2 trillion student loan market? Suppose a major financial institution, such as a pension firm or an insurance company (both crushed by low interest rates), goes under? I think there are several ways in which another financial crisis could kick off.

Given the Fed's refusal to allow defaults or market declines, we can expect that they'd respond by again pouring money into the system and removing even more rules. But that trick can't work every time. The United States is the world's reserve currency, despite the fact that we're the world's largest debtor and that we severed any real backing of assets for the dollar when Nixon took us off the gold standard in 1971.

If the U.S. were a closed system, they could probably get away with this for a long time: We don't have any alternatives to the dollar. But the world's view is very different. People in other countries already know that there's nothing backing the dollar, and they already hold a lot of dollars and dollar-denominated assets (like Treasury bonds) based on the idea that it still serves as a store of value. If they see the Fed make another large-scale move to shore up domestic markets with a further infusion of dollars created from thin air, they have a strong motivation to get rid of those devaluing dollars—and to do so quickly, before they lose more value.

If foreign markets start to abandon the U.S. dollar, the effect at home would be cataclysmic. First, people overseas wouldn't want dollar-denominated assets anymore, leading to a sell-off in Treasury bonds and a refusal to buy more American debt, largely eliminating our ability to run deficits; as a result, interest rates would rise rapidly to make them more attractive to the few buyers left. If the Fed stepped in to buy that debt the problem would get exponentially worse. Even beyond the debt issue, foreigners would try to get rid of any dollars they had left, resulting in a flood of dollars coming into the country as people tried to exchange them in a panic for real goods.

The result of this huge influx of dollars will be hyperinflation, with the dollar rapidly losing what little value it had left. Our days of running deficits will be over, since no one will accept devalued dollars for their products, which will be a problem particularly for things like oil. (Despite what you hear from the media, we are not energy independent.)

With all those dollars flowing back in, you'd think we'd all be awash in money; we wouldn't be. As prices rise rapidly, demand falls off, which means people will lose their jobs. We'll end up with hyperinflation in the things we need, and since few will be able to afford luxury items, we'll see widespread deflation in the things we want, such as all those assets that retirees need to sell.

The social impact of these changes will be severe. There's already quite a bit of resentment against the rich and powerful; that will increase as they'll be blamed for these problems, and that may turn into some unpleasant actions. Government programs like Social Security and Medicare will fail to provide for people's basic needs, and those who cannot provide for themselves, like the elderly, will find themselves in severe distress. The rest of us will struggle to get by with little money and out-of-reach prices. It will be the Great Depression all over again, even though the Fed was specifically trying to avoid that outcome. And what's worse, we'll be living in a Great Depression without the skills and self-sufficiency that allowed our forebears to survive it.

I want to reiterate that this is just one possible scenario; it's just what I personally see as being likely, and the future may play out in a completely different fashion. But I think when you consider all of the challenges listed at the start of this chapter, it's hard to envision a scenario where everything turns out just fine.

AN ALTERNATE VIEW

A disruption doesn't have to come from government overreaction, and it doesn't have to be caused by an inflationary spike. It could also come from an extension of existing consumer behavior, leading directly to deflation without the extra steps suggested above.

In economic terms, deflation refers to a reduction in the money supply; in practical terms, we would experience it as a vicious spiral with purchasing ability and product pricing ratcheting lower and lower. (Imagine consumers spending less, which leads to lower prices as companies try to capture any remaining customers, which leads to consumers spending even less as they either lose their jobs or wait for prices to drop even further.)

The elements for a deflationary slide are largely already in place. The labor participation rate hasn't been this low since the 1970s, meaning there are a lot fewer people generating income than there have been in recent decades. And with the prices of a handful of needs continuing to rise rapidly, particularly healthcare, those people who do have incomes have far fewer dollars to spend on other things.

We're already seeing a muted level of deflation now, with intense price competition for goods and services along with a shakeout in the retail sector. To kick off a more pronounced and rapid deflation, all we would need is a continuation of trends, such as a continued increase in healthcare premiums (which would also lead to more employers dropping plans and leaving employees to shoulder the entire burden) or a sudden additional stress on purchasing power, such as lower wages from a recession or a move to tighten credit standards, leaving people with less credit.

Once you enter a true deflationary cycle, it's very hard to escape. People with less income not only spend less, hurting the commercial economy, but pay less in taxes, hurting government revenues (which in turn again hurts the economy through lower levels of government spending and less money available for public welfare payments). After a few rounds of this type of deflationary cycle we would end up in a second Great Depression, traveling a different path to the same outcome from the previous hypothetical example.

WHEN WILL SOMETHING HAPPEN?

Imagine that it's 2002, and you live in New Orleans, in St. Bernard Parish. You know your Parish sits below sea level, and you know that storm activity has increased over the past few years. You start to do some research, and it becomes clear to you that it's only a matter of time before a big storm hits your area and, thanks to your location, the effects could be extremely bad.

Armed with that information, what would you do? Would you make plans to move from an inherently dangerous situation, even if you don't know when that danger might occur? Would you warn your friends and neighbors, or worry that they would think you an alarmist—or worse? If someone offered you an opportunity to invest in local real estate—making a long-term investment in the area—would you do it? Or would you dismiss what you had read and just go on living your life, reasoning that since nothing bad had happened so far, everything was probably fine?

If you tried to tell people what you learned, you might forgive them for not believing you—life went on, Mardi Gras came and went every year, and nothing actually happened. Nothing, that is, until August 29, 2005, when New Orleans was hit by Hurricane Katrina—and St. Bernard Parish, your home, was under 12 feet of water within minutes of the levee breaking.

This may be a dramatic analogy—but I think it's a fair one, and it makes an important point. No one can predict when something bad will happen. But if you see all of the trends leading inevitably to that point, then you have time to prepare for it. You don't know how much time you have—it could be a day, it could be ten years—but you do have time, and it's your responsibility to use it wisely. The question of "when" is of lesser importance if you have a clear sense of "what." Every day is a chance to do something to help you weather the storm that you know is coming.

As the old saying goes, "Better a year early than a day late."

17

WHAT YOU CAN DO ABOUT IT

In an age of universal deceit, telling the truth is a revolutionary act.

—Unknown; often attributed to George Orwell

> **THE POINT:**
>
> Yes, the cards are stacked against you. But that's only if you play their game, by their rules. It's time to play your own game.

As I was sharing early drafts of this book with a few people, most had the same reaction: "Things look pretty bad! I can't wait to see your recommendations for fixing it." If you're looking for solutions, however, I hate to disappoint you, but I don't have any.

As Chris Martenson of the popular website Peak Prosperity often notes, there is a difference between a problem and a predicament. A problem is something that can be fixed; a predicament is something you can't fix and just have to find a way to deal with. Being in debt is a problem; you can solve it by spending less and/or earning more, and using every available penny to pay off that debt. It may be uncomfortable, and it may take a while, but you can solve that problem. Death is a predicament;

you can't change it, so you just have to come to terms with it, and get as much meaning and happiness from your life as you can in the limited time you have on this planet.

If we were only faced with one of the issues mentioned in this book, we could find a solution. If the money and financial systems were sound and government was trustworthy and effective, for example, we could root out problems in the corporate arena. But that's not where we are. There is too much corruption and too much dysfunction in too many of the major institutions of this country, and it is so deeply rooted that there is no way we can fix it all.

As an example, many people believe that Congressional term limits would help. But what is the likelihood that 535 career politicians are going to vote themselves out of a job? And if they do, won't they just end up in lobbying roles, trading on their contact lists? And what about our record-breaking $20 trillion in federal debt? Even if we're able to reduce the annual deficit to zero, what's the likelihood that we'll be able to pay that debt down given our economic challenges and the increased social needs of our retiring Boomers?

Clearly, what we have is a predicament, and not just a problem. But that doesn't mean that you should be despondent. On the contrary, the ability to see reality can be incredibly empowering. In his landmark book, *Good to Great*, Jim Collins writes about the Stockdale Paradox, describing how Admiral James Stockdale was able to survive for eight years as a prisoner during the Vietnam War.

Stockdale held an unshakeable faith that he would survive the prison camps, that he would see his wife again, and that this experience would be the defining event in his life. But he did not hold out false hope, thinking he could just sit and wait to be rescued.

He noted that the prisoners who were the most optimistic were actually the ones who failed to survive: He said that "They were the ones who said, 'We're going to be out by Christmas.' And Christmas would come, and Christmas would go. Then they'd say, 'We're going to be out by Easter.' And Easter would come, and Easter would go. And then Thanksgiving, and then it would be Christmas again. And they died of a broken heart."[331]

Rather than sit and hope, as the doomed optimists did, Stockdale acknowledged his reality and did what he could to survive, fight back, and hold on. He comforted other prisoners; he tried to send intelligence information out in the letters he wrote to his wife; he thought about ways to help people resist the torture so many endured. In short, even though he was powerless to change his overall situation, he held on to his incredibly strong faith that he would ultimately make it through, and took every action he could so that he and his fellow soldiers could survive and resist.

That, ultimately, is my advice to you. I ask that you acknowledge the fact that the institutions within our lives are beyond fixing, but that you maintain absolute resolve that we will make it through to a new day one way or another. And in the meantime, I ask that you take actions to survive, resist, and hold on until that day ultimately comes.

WHAT CAN YOU DO?

At the beginning of this book, I offered the idea that a fish has no idea it's in water: Our environment (in our case, the rules we live by, and the systems we operate within), are invisible to us.

So what would happen if a fish suddenly realized that it was surrounded by water—and that water was polluted? If it were smart, the fish would either find some way to clean the water, or move elsewhere to where the water was livable.

I'm not advocating that you move somewhere else, though you're certainly free to do so if that's your judgment. As for me, I'm staying here: Even with all the problems we have, I belong here. I believe that the vast majority of people in this country are good people who want to do the right thing and will join together as a community when we face challenges. And I think this country's founding principles are good ones, ones we can return to if we try.

So the answer, to me, is to clean your own water—make your own life livable. You don't have to fix the entire system—it would be impossible for that fish to clean the ocean—but if you can set up your own living environment and lifestyle to have a healthy and productive life, free (to the extent possible) of the corruption that surrounds us, that's probably the best you can shoot for.

So what can you do to live your best life, a life as free as possible from the manipulative and unfair system that has grown so large?

STAY WITHIN THE LAW

First things first: Don't do anything illegal. If you feel that banks are robbing you, there may be a temptation to rob them back; if you feel the government is stealing from you, there may be a temptation to cheat on your taxes. Don't.

Live an honorable life, and understand that it's good to unplug from the system, and it's good to leverage the rules of the system in your favor; it's very bad to break the rules of the system, because the ones who suffer most if you get caught are you and those you love. Better to stay peaceful and stay legal.

EDUCATE YOURSELF

This book is little more than a pamphlet, scratching the surface on things that would take months or years to fully explore. It's a starting point presented by one person; your job now is to look for other sources that confirm or deny what's written here, and expand your understanding of the issues that you most want to grasp.

CONFORMITY

There's a huge amount of peer pressure out there to think what everyone else thinks, even if you realize that it's wrong. The government, the schools, the media, and even your friends all tell you similar stories: The TSA is there to keep us safe, our military is fighting for our freedom, you have to get a college degree if you want to succeed in life, and so on. Don't abandon your knowledge and beliefs just based on the number of people who believe something different; the crowd is not always right.

But on the flip side, don't expect everyone else to understand what you've come to understand. It's fine to share your thinking with others; in fact I'd encourage you to do so, especially with those who are important to you. But if they don't buy in, then let them be. Normalcy bias, and the voice of the crowd, are very powerful; they'll find their way eventually, and when they do you'll want them to feel comfortable coming to you when they're ready.

GET RID OF DEBT

Remember back to the first section in this book: The money system, and the financial industry, lives on debt—it's what gives them their power, specifically their power over you. Don't let them. Pay off debt as fast as possible, and don't take any new debt. You'll stop losing money to interest payments, and you'll gain a tremendous sense of freedom when you don't have that debt hanging over you. It's hard, but it's a huge step in getting your life back.

BUY REAL THINGS

If you're able to invest, understand that the potential for a crash in the financial markets is very high right now, so buying stocks, bonds, and other types of investments could result in you losing a lot of your money. The alternative is to buy real assets, things that have value no matter what happens in the financial markets. That would include precious metals, real estate, farmland, and investing in the tools and skills you need to live self-sufficiently.

DON'T BE MAD AT THE WRONG PEOPLE

Try to make the distinction between the people who set up unjust systems and the people who work within them. Just because the banks are engaged in illegal and unethical behavior, that doesn't mean your local teller or branch manager is in on it or benefits from it in the same way the bank CEO does. Just because the education system pushes a fraudulent model like Common Core, that doesn't mean your child's teacher is part of the scam. Remember that most of the people who work in these fields are just like you: Trying to do what's right and take care of their families. Unless proven otherwise, they don't deserve your anger.

THINK THROUGH YOUR PRIORITIES

We've been told throughout our lives that if we want to be happy, we need more, and we need bigger: More money, more clothes, a nicer car, a bigger house. And sure, those things are all nice. But think carefully: Are they worth the price that you have to pay for them? You might be able to acquire all of those things, but are they worth the debt servitude, and committing to a job that you hate for the rest of your life? Or can you be happy with simpler things, if they're accompanied by the freedom of not having debt, and being able to find work you enjoy (or even working less so you have more free time)? More and better is not always the answer—you can make a different choice.

DO IT YOURSELF

Fifty or a hundred years ago, people were fairly self-sufficient; they knew how to do things. They could change their own oil, grow their own food (or at least some of it), sew or at least mend their own clothes, and do their own home repairs. Today we're much more likely to pay for all of those things rather than do them ourselves, either because we don't have time or we don't have the knowledge or skills. But maybe it's time to start learning how to do things again.

You don't have to go buy a cabin in the woods and live off-grid; just start small and see firsthand what a difference it makes in the quality of your life and your feeling of independence. Learn to sew. Grow a few vegetables. Learn how to change your oil. Learn how to replace a light fixture. Cook a meal. It doesn't matter what you do—if you can figure out how to do things yourself, the confidence and sense of empowerment will carry over into other parts of your life. And as a bonus, you'll save money—perhaps a lot of money—and start to get off the consumer treadmill.

FIND A COMMUNITY

One of the best things about the internet is that it allows us to connect with people based on our beliefs and interests without being limited by where we live. If you can find like-minded people locally, that's fantastic! If not, look for those people online; there are lots of sites and online communities for you if you just look for them. Remember that you're looking for a community, not just an echo chamber. You want people you can share your thoughts with and who you can learn from, but you should also try hard to expose yourself to other thinking as well. You want to continue learning and evolving, and that can't happen if you're with people you agree with 100 percent of the time.

But beyond finding people who share your beliefs, you would be well-served to become fully involved in your local community, including your neighborhood, your local government, and area affinity groups (your child's PTA, a gardening club, your church). No one is an island; if and when hard times appear, you'll want to surround yourself with people who you know and trust, people who can band together to share resources and tackle any challenges. Community members pass along children's clothes as they grow; they let you borrow an expensive but seldom-used tool; they're ready to help when you're missing an ingredient or even when you need a meal. It's how many survived the last Great Depression; it's also how many will survive the next.

LIVE YOUR LIFE

I'll admit that when I first started to figure out how broken our system is, I panicked a little and started thinking about worst-case scenarios, like a "Mad Max" lifestyle resulting from a total breakdown in society. It's the kind of thing that makes you want to stockpile essential supplies and get a compound in the mountains! But let's be realistic: We may go through some rough times, like they did in the Great Depression, but those times are temporary and they're useful as a way to wash out the problems and give us a fresh start as a society. Remember that the Great Depression didn't last forever, it wasn't a total breakdown (even at its height, 75 percent were still employed),[332] and it led into one of the greatest periods of prosperity the world has ever known.

So don't build that bomb shelter, and don't buy that fortified compound. Educate yourself and prepare yourself, but don't let the future consume you. Live your life, love your spouse and kids and spend time with them, enjoy your hobbies, and appreciate all that you have. Yes, we face real challenges, but don't sacrifice yourself to your worries—live, and love, your life right now.

Again, none of the suggestions here are intended to fix the huge problems we see in this country; I honestly don't know of a way to change the direction things are going, and point them toward a system that works for the majority of us. These ideas are just to help you live the best life you can: Make a conscious effort to define happiness and live a real, happy, and sustainable life. And I think that's about all we can do.

ENDNOTES

1   http://www.archives.gov/exhibits/charters/constitution_transcript.html
2   http://www.factcheck.org/2008/03/federal-reserve-bank-ownership/
3   https://mises.org/library/losing-battle-fix-gold-35
4   http://www.inflationdata.com/inflation/Consumer_Price_Index/Historical CPI.aspx?reloaded=true
5   https://peakprosperity.com/blog/104753/2016-year-review
6   https://research.stlouisfed.org/fred2/series/TCMDO
7   http://www.zerohedge.com/news/2015-03-10/happy-6th-birthday-day-fasb-folded-mark-fantasy-was-born
8   http://video.cnbc.com/gallery/?video=3000474362
9   http://nypost.com/2014/10/20/plunge-protection-behind-markets-sudden-recovery/
10 https://www.federalreserve.gov/monetarypolicy/files/quarterly_balance _sheet_developments_report_201611.pdf
11 http://www.cjr.org/the_audit/the_too_big_to_fail_banks_stil.php
12 https://katusaresearch.com/what-will-happen-to-all-the-debt-in-the-oil-patch/
13 http://www.zerohedge.com/news/2016-08-09/james-grant-negative-interest-rates-will-end-badly
14 http://www.wsj.com/articles/share-buybacks-the-bill-is-coming-due-1456685173
15 http://blogs.wsj.com/washwire/2013/03/06/holder-banks-may-be-too-large-to-prosecute/
16 http://www.goodjobsfirst.org/sites/default/files/docs/pdf /160billionbankfee.pdf
17 http://www.latimes.com/business/la-fi-mo-hsbc-senate-20120717-story.html

18 https://www.theguardian.com/world/2011/apr/03/us-bank-mexico-drug-gangs

19 https://www.fdic.gov/about/strategic/corporate/cfo_report_1stqtr_16/balance.html

20 https://fred.stlouisfed.org/series/DPSACBW027SBOG

21 http://www.zerohedge.com/news/2016-04-14/markets-are-manipulated

22 https://www.bloomberg.com/news/articles/2015-06-09/the-alleged-flash-trading-mastermind-lived-with-his-parents-and-couldn-t-drive

23 http://www.telegraph.co.uk/news/2016/11/09/british-flash-crash-trader-navinder-sarao-pleads-guilty-in-us-to/

24 http://www.bis.org/statistics/d5_1.pdf

25 https://www.cia.gov/library/publications/the-world-factbook/geos/xx.html

26 https://www.usnews.com/news/articles/2008/05/29/the-pact-between-bill-clinton-and-newt-gingrich

27 https://www.brookings.edu/research/why-the-2005-social-security-initiative-failed-and-what-it-means-for-the-future/

28 http://www.politico.com/blogs/2016-presidential-debate-fact-check/2016/10/mike-pence-social-security-privatize-bush-229140

29 http://money.cnn.com/2016/11/21/news/economy/kfile-trump-social-security/index.html

30 https://www.justice.gov/criminal-fraud/identity-theft/identity-theft-and-identity-fraud

31 http://www.nytimes.com/2016/09/27/business/dealbook/wells-fargo-workers-claim-retaliation-for-playing-by-the-rules.html

32 https://assets.bwbx.io/documents/users/iqjWHBFdfxIU/rPxi_pVaKx2Y/v0

33 http://www.nytimes.com/2016/10/12/business/dealbook/at-wells-fargo-complaints-about-fraudulent-accounts-since-2005.html?_r=2

34 http://www.nytimes.com/2016/09/27/business/dealbook/wells-fargo-workers-claim-retaliation-for-playing-by-the-rules.html

35 http://www.wsj.com/articles/wells-fargo-ceo-defends-bank-culture-lays-blame-with-bad-employees-1473784452

36 http://www.nytimes.com/2016/11/19/business/regulator-tightens-control-over-wells-fargo.html

37 http://www.nasdaq.com/article/wells-fargo-account-opening-plunges-44-post-sales-scam-cm711527

38 https://www.goodreads.com/book/show/7830370-how-the-west-was-lost

39 https://www.washingtonpost.com/realestate/by-not-downsizing-baby-

boomers-help-clog-up-the-real-estate-pipeline/2015/12/01/ec88299e-978f-11e5-b499-76cbec161973_story.html?utm_term=.cbd91402270d

40 http://www.aei.org/publication/todays-new-homes-are-1000-square-feet-larger-than-in-1973-and-the-living-space-per-person-has-doubled-over-last-40-years/

41 https://www.washingtonpost.com/realestate/by-not-downsizing-baby-boomers-help-clog-up-the-real-estate-pipeline/2015/12/01/ec88299e-978f-11e5-b499-76cbec161973_story.html?utm_term=.cbd91402270d

42 http://www.fanniemae.com/resources/file/research/datanotes/pdf/housing-insights-082015.pdf

43 http://www.theatlantic.com/national/archive/2014/03/here-is-when-each-generation-begins-and-ends-according-to-facts/359589/

44 https://www.bloomberg.com/news/articles/2015-06-10/millennials-think-they-have-it-bad-generation-x-has-it-worse

45 https://www.stlouisfed.org/publications/in-the-balance/issue9-2014/despite-aggressive-deleveraging-generation-x-remains-generation-debt

46 http://www.businessinsider.com/americas-crushing-student-debt-has-bred-a-disturbing-new-phenomenon-2015-10

47 http://www.pewsocialtrends.org/2016/05/24/for-first-time-in-modern-era-living-with-parents-edges-out-other-living-arrangements-for-18-to-34-year-olds/

48 https://www.bloomberg.com/news/articles/2015-12-03/reasons-to-be-skeptical-about-a-millennial-homebuying-boom-in-2016

49 https://fred.stlouisfed.org/series/MORTGAGE30US

50 https://www.uvu.edu/woodbury/docs/summaryoftheprimarycauseofthe-housingbubble.pdf

51 https://fred.stlouisfed.org/series/ASPUS

52 http://lasvegassun.com/news/2010/jun/11/building-boom-recessionary-bust-local-real-estate-/

53 http://www.nytimes.com/2009/12/24/business/24trading.html?page-wanted=all

54 http://www.mcclatchydc.com/news/politics-government/article24561376.html

55 https://www.uvu.edu/woodbury/docs/summaryoftheprimarycauseofthe-housingbubble.pdf

56 http://www.wsj.com/articles/big-banks-paid-110-billionin-mortgage-related-fines-where-did-the-money-go-1457557442

57 http://www.cnbc.com/2015/10/06/housing-today-a-bubble-larger-than-2006.html

58 http://www.fool.com/retirement/general/2016/05/08/the-average-american-household-owes-90336-how-do-y.aspx

59 https://www.census.gov/people/wealth/data/debttables.html

60 http://libertystreeteconomics.newyorkfed.org/2016/02/the-graying-of-american-debt.html (data tables)

61 https://www.census.gov/people/wealth/data/dtables.html

62 http://www.fool.com/investing/general/2015/05/25/the-typical-american-has-this-much-in-home-equity.aspx

63 Ibid.

64 https://www.census.gov/prod/2002pubs/censr-4.pdf page 59
https://www.census.gov/prod/cen2010/briefs/c2010br-03.pdf
https://www.census.gov/population/projections/data/national/2014/summarytables.html

65 http://www.cbsnews.com/news/will-retiring-baby-boomers-lead-to-a-stock-market-bust/

66 https://www.washingtonpost.com/news/storyline/wp/2014/09/19/whats-eating-generations-xs-wealth/?utm_term=.e27ff515b2a7

67 https://www.cato.org/publications/commentary/is-there-right-social-security

68 http://www.agewave.com/media_files/commonGround.pdf

69 https://www.ssa.gov/oact/trsum/

70 https://www.ssa.gov/OACT/ProgData/fundFAQ.html

71 http://www.forbes.com/sites/merrillmatthews/2011/07/13/what-happened-to-the-2-6-trillion-social-security-trust-fund/#60b153af6153

72 http://www.gallup.com/poll/182921/nonretirees-expect-rely-social-security.aspx?utm_source=alert&utm_medium=email&utm_content=morelink&utm_campaign=syndication

73 http://kff.org/medicare/issue-brief/an-overview-of-medicare/

74 http://kff.org/medicare/issue-brief/the-facts-on-medicare-spending-and-financing/

75 http://www.epi.org/blog/private-sector-pension-coverage-decline/

76 http://www.heritage.org/research/reports/2015/07/bankrupt-pensions-and-insolvent-pension-insurance-the-case-of-multiemployer-pensions-and-the-pbgcs-multiemployer-program

77 http://www.pbgc.gov/documents/2014-data-tables-final.pdf

78 http://www.pbgc.gov/documents/2014-ERISA-Section-4010-Report-and-cover-letter-12-20-2016.pdf

79 http://www.pewtrusts.org/en/research-and-analysis/issue-briefs/2016/08/the-state-pension-funding-gap-2014

80 http://www.forbes.com/sites/andrewbiggs/2016/07/01/are-state-and-local-government-pensions-underfunded-by-5-trillion/#55b4e9c37c8f

81 https://www.aei.org/wp-content/uploads/2014/03/-aei-economic-perspective-march-2014_160053300510.pdf

82 http://www.wsj.com/articles/SB1000142405270230483010457517226290979 4220

83 http://www.marketwatch.com/story/you-could-be-on-the-hook-for-pension-funds-lofty-stock-market-views-2015-05-15

84 http://www.latimes.com/business/la-fi-stockton-pension-court-ruling-cuts-20141029-story.html

85 http://www.reuters.com/article/bankruptcy-sanbernardino-agreement-idUSL2N15J03S

86 http://www.zerohedge.com/news/2016-04-20/going-be-national-crisis-one-largest-us-pension-funds-set-cut-retiree-benefits

87 http://www.dallasnews.com/opinion/editorials/2016/11/28/dallas-state-legislature-step-help-fix-police-fire-pension-fund

88 https://www.creditcards.com/credit-card-news/interest-rate-report-101117-unchanged-2121.php

89 https://www.nerdwallet.com/blog/insurance/life-insurance-agent-commissions/

90 http://www.wsj.com/articles/SB10001424052702303296604577450313299530278

91 https://www.ftc.gov/news-events/media-resources/consumer-finance/pay-day-lending

92 https://www.fdic.gov/about/strategic/corporate/cfo_report_1stqtr_16/balance.html

93 https://fred.stlouisfed.org/series/DPSACBW027SBOG

94 https://www.ft.com/content/80e2987a-2e50-11dc-821c-0000779fd2ac

95 http://www.nytimes.com/2008/09/25/business/25voices.html?_r=0

96 http://www.politico.com/story/2008/10/the-senate-bailout-vote-014196

97 http://www.cbsnews.com/news/poll-talk-first-fight-later/

98 http://scholar.princeton.edu/sites/default/files/mgilens/files/gilens_and_page_2014_-testing_theories_of_american_politics.doc.pdf

99 http://www.opensecrets.org/politicians/

100 https://www.techdirt.com/articles/20130416/08344222725/congress-quickly-quietly-rolls-back-insider-trading-rules-itself.shtml

101 https://www.propublica.org/article/do-as-we-say-congress-says-then-does-what-it-wants

102 http://www.forbes.com/sites/larrybell/2013/12/22/unions-get-big-obamacare-

christmas-present-as-other-self-insured-groups-get-scrooged/#2fa
f8906baa0

103 https://www.washingtonpost.com/news/the-switch/wp/2016/07/06/why-
companies-cant-spam-you-with-robocalls-but-the-government-can/

104 http://www.theamericanmirror.com/nancy-pelosi-driver-cuts-across-traffic/

105 http://www.cnn.com/2014/03/13/politics/feinstein-cia-snooping-hypocrisy
/index.html

106 https://www.census.gov/prod/cen2010/briefs/c2010br-08.pdf

107 http://www.politifact.com/truth-o-meter/statements/2014/nov/11/face-
book-posts/congress-has-11-approval-ratings-96-incumbent-re-e/

108 http://www.gallup.com/poll/1597/confidence-institutions.aspx

109 http://www.uspirg.org/news/usp/better-funded-candidates-sweep-con-
gressional-primaries

110 http://www.usnews.com/news/the-report/articles/2016-02-19/americas-
primary-elections-are-broken

111 http://www.huffingtonpost.com/entry/wikileaks-emails-show-dnc-favored-
hillary-clinton-over_us_57930be0e4b0e002a3134b05

112 https://www.democracynow.org/2012/8/29/chaos_on_the_convention_floor
_as

113 https://en.wikipedia.org/wiki/List_of_political_parties_in_the_United_
States

114 http://www.usatoday.com/story/news/politics/onpolitics/2016/08/31/poll-
clinton-trump-most-unfavorable-candidates-ever/89644296/

115 https://www.washingtonpost.com/news/the-fix/wp/2016/04/27/why-are-
there-only-two-parties-in-american-politics/?utm_term=.a84dd8ea8b4d

116 http://www.huffingtonpost.com/pete-tucker/what-the-hell-how-third-
p_b_11277474.html

117 http://www.pbs.org/newshour/updates/americas-off-love-affair-third-
party-candidates/

118 https://www.nytimes.com/interactive/2016/10/21/us/elections/television-ads
.html

119 http://www.peakprosperity.com/video/85854/playlist/92161/crash-course-
chapter-18-fuzzy-numbers

120 http://www.marketplace.org/2013/04/22/economy/us-economy-grow-
3-under-new-gdp-calculation

121 http://www.zerohedge.com/news/2015-11-06/most-surprising-thing-
about-todays-jobs-report

122 https://www.washingtonpost.com/business/on-small-business/more-businesses

-are-closing-than-starting-can-congress-help-turn-that-around/2014/09/17/065
76cb8-385a-11e4-8601-97ba88884ffd_story.html

123 https://fred.stlouisfed.org/series/LNU01300000

124 https://obamawhitehouse.archives.gov/sites/default/files/omb/budget/fy2017
/assets/hist.pdf

125 https://www.treasurydirect.gov/NP/debt/current

126 Actual deficit calculated from year-over-year comparisons from the Treasury
Department's "Debt to the Penny" reports

127 https://www.bls.gov/cpi/cpifaq.htm#Question_1

128 http://www.forbes.com/sites/perianneboring/2014/02/03/if-you-want-to-
know-the-real-rate-of-inflation-dont-bother-with-the-cpi/#30a361ba118b

129 http://www.zerohedge.com/news/2014-11-14/manipulation-cpi-saved-federal
-government-over-150-billion-1998-2012

130 http://www.chapwoodindex.com/

131 Ibid.

132 http://www.nytimes.com/2010/08/03/opinion/03geithner.html?_r=0

133 http://www.npr.org/sections/money/2009/03/bernanke_sees_green_shoots
.html

134 http://www.zerohedge.com/news/2015-09-16/obamas-recovery-just-
9-charts

135 http://www.huffingtonpost.com/max-galka/in-2015-the-government-
se_b_9666772.html

136 http://www.msn.com/en-us/news/us/theft-of-ancient-bones-a-debacle-for-
national-park-service/ar-AAi5m7W?ocid=ansmsnnews11

137 http://www.oftwominds.com/blog.html

138 http://www.newsweek.com/2014/10/24/when-it-comes-beheadings-isis-
has-nothing-over-saudi-arabia-277385.html

139 https://www.hrw.org/world-report/2015/country-chapters/saudi-arabia

140 https://en.wikipedia.org/wiki/LGBT_rights_in_Saudi_Arabia

141 http://www.cfr.org/china/chinas-environmental-crisis/p12608

142 http://chinalaborwatch.org/home.aspx

143 http://www.apfn.org/THEWINDS/1997/05/favored_china.html

144 http://fair.org/home/outlets-that-scolded-sanders-over-deficits-uniformly-
silent-on-700b-pentagon-handout/

145 http://blog.tsa.gov/2010/12/70-detection-failure-rate-being.html

146 http://www.cnn.com/2015/06/01/politics/tsa-failed-undercover-airport-
screening-tests/index.html

147 http://www.cnn.com/2014/05/23/politics/va-scandals-timeline/index.html

148 http://www.washingtonsblog.com/2013/10/americans-have-lost-virtually-all-of-our-constitutional-rights.html

149 http://www.news9.com/story/32168555/ohp-uses-new-device-to-seize-money-used-during-the-commission-of-a-crime

150 http://www.nytimes.com/2015/06/05/opinion/edward-snowden-the-world-says-no-to-surveillance.html

151 http://www.nationalreview.com/article/448942/asset-forfeiture-police-abuse-it-all-time

152 https://www.theatlantic.com/politics/archive/2017/07/sessions-forfeiture-justice-department-civil/534168/

153 http://www.sfgate.com/technology/businessinsider/article/US-Government-Funded-Domestic-Propaganda-Has-4668001.php

154 http://www.zerohedge.com/news/2016-12-10/senate-quietly-passes-countering-disinformation-and-propaganda-act

155 http://books.sipri.org/files/FS/SIPRIFS1604.pdf

156 https://en.wikipedia.org/wiki/List_of_countries_by_number_of_military_and_paramilitary_personnel

157 http://www.politico.com/magazine/story/2015/06/us-military-bases-around-the-world-119321

158 https://www.thenation.com/article/the-united-states-probably-has-more-foreign-military-bases-than-any-other-people-nation-or-empire-in-history/

159 http://www.acq.osd.mil/eie/Downloads/BSI/Base percent20Structure percent20Report percent20FY15.pdf

160 https://www.defense.gov/About-DoD

161 https://www.youtube.com/watch?v=SXS3vW47mOE

162 https://www.foreignaffairs.com/articles/libya/obamas-libya-debacle

163 https://www.theguardian.com/commentisfree/2017/jan/09/america-dropped-26171-bombs-2016-obama-legacy

164 http://blogs.cfr.org/zenko/2017/01/05/bombs-dropped-in-2016/

165 http://www.opensecrets.org/lobby/top.php?showYear=2015&indexType=i

166 http://www.military.com/daily-news/2015/01/28/pentagon-tells-congress-to-stop-buying-equipment-it-doesnt-need.html

167 http://archive.boston.com/news/nation/washington/articles/2010/12/26/defense_firms_lure_retired_generals/?page=2

168 http://www.cbsnews.com/news/the-war-on-waste/

169 http://www.cnn.com/2016/08/23/politics/us-army-audit-accounting-errors/

170 https://www.washingtonpost.com/investigations/pentagon-buries-evidence-of-125-billion-in-bureaucratic-waste/2016/12/05/e0668c76-9af6-11e6-a0ed-ab0774c1eaa5_story.html?utm_term=.487f358dc20b

171 http://www.telegraph.co.uk/news/worldnews/asia/afghanistan/11211358/
     US-army-loses-military-equipment-worth-420-million-in-Afghanistan
     .html

172 https://www.washingtonpost.com/world/national-security/pentagon-loses-
     sight-of-500-million-in-counterterrorism-aid-given-to-yemen/2015/03/17/
     f4ca25ce-cbf9-11e4-8a46-b1dc9be5a8ff_story.html?utm_
     term=.97df3d0c21f4

173 Did not satisfy the requirements necessary to earn an undergraduate degree.

174 https://www.washingtonpost.com/politics/how-bill-gates-pulled-off-the-
     swift-common-core-revolution/2014/06/07/a830e32e-ec34-11e3-9f5c-
     9075d5508f0a_story.html

175 http://news.heartland.org/newspaper-article/2013/06/07/five-people-
     wrote-state-led-common-core

176 http://www.uaedreform.org/wp-content/uploads/2000/01/ZimbaMilgram
     StotskyFinal.pdf

177 http://pioneerinstitute.org/news/lowering-the-bar-how-common-core-
     math-fails-to-prepare-students-for-stem/

178 http://files.eric.ed.gov/fulltext/ED539373.pdf

179 https://www.usatoday.com/story/money/2017/08/21/10-in-demand-jobs-
     workers-without-bachelors-degree/585960001/

180 https://ggwash.org/view/39036/some-are-questioning-whether-all-students-
     should-be-on-a-college-prep-track

181 http://hechingerreport.org/college-for-all-vs-career-education-moving-
     beyond-a-false-debate/

182 http://www.huffingtonpost.com/2013/06/14/college-costs-median-income
     _n_3443806.html

183 http://economix.blogs.nytimes.com/2012/03/02/why-tuition-has-skyrocketed
     -at-state-schools/

184 http://www.csmonitor.com/Business/2010/0330/Student-loan-reform-
     What-will-it-mean-for-students

185 https://fred.stlouisfed.org/series/SLOAS

186 http://www.fool.com/investing/general/2015/01/24/the-average-american
     -owes-this-much-in-student-loa.aspx

187 http://www.consumerfinance.gov/about-us/newsroom/cfpb-concerned-
     about-widespread-servicing-failures-reported-by-student-loan-borrowers/

188 http://www.cnbc.com/2015/06/15/the-high-economic-and-social-costs-of-
     student-loan-debt.html

189 https://en.wikipedia.org/wiki/Bankruptcy_Abuse_Prevention_and_Consumer_Protection_Act

190 http://americanradioworks.publicradio.org/features/tomorrows-college/phoenix/story-of-university-of-phoenix.html

191 http://billmoyers.com/story/the-for-profit-college-scam-that-these-students-are-still-paying-for/

192 https://www.usnews.com/opinion/blogs/carrie-wofford/2013/11/11/this-veterans-day-help-a-vet-avoid-a-gi-bill-for-profit-college-scam

193 https://www.archives.gov/founding-docs/declaration-transcript

194 https://www.archives.gov/founding-docs/bill-of-rights-transcript

195 http://www.washingtontimes.com/news/2016/oct/6/liberal-professors-outnumber-conservatives-12-1/

196 https://www.nytimes.com/2016/05/08/opinion/sunday/a-confession-of-liberal-intolerance.html

197 https://www.insidehighered.com/news/2016/03/30/new-book-details-realities-being-conservative-professor-humanities-and-social

198 http://www.businessinsider.com/list-of-disinvited-speakers-at-colleges-2016-7

199 http://time.com/4530197/college-free-speech-zone/

200 https://en.wikipedia.org/wiki/Free_speech_zone

201 http://www.aljazeera.com/indepth/opinion/2013/06/201362574347243214.html

202 https://www.washingtonpost.com/news/volokh-conspiracy/wp/2015/10/06/zero-correlation-between-state-homicide-rate-and-state-gun-laws/?utm_term=.1f5eadb50e6a

203 http://www.nationalreview.com/article/425802/gun-free-zones-don percent27t-save-lives-right-to-carry-laws-do

204 https://www.archives.gov/founding-docs/declaration-transcript

205 https://www.defense.gov/News/Special-Reports/FY16-Budget

206 https://www.pri.org/stories/2013-07-09/17-disturbing-things-snowden-has-taught-us-so-far

207 http://www.theregister.co.uk/2015/12/07/reason_clapper_lied_about_nsa_spying/

208 http://www.motherjones.com/mojo/2013/06/fisa-court-nsa-spying-opinion-reject-request

209 https://www.bloomberg.com/features/2016-baltimore-secret-surveillance/

210 http://www.slate.com/articles/news_and_politics/jurisprudence/2013/06/

salinas_v_texas_right_to_remain_silent_supreme_court_right_to_
remain_silent.html

211 http://www.washingtonpost.com/sf/investigative/2014/09/06/stop-and-
seize/

212 http://www.fed-soc.org/blog/detail/no-fly-no-buy-and-no-due-process

213 http://abovethelaw.com/2015/06/underfunding-public-defenders-can-
lead-to-sixth-amendment-violations/

214 https://www.theatlantic.com/magazine/archive/2017/09/innocence-is-
irrelevant/534171/

215 http://hardnoxandfriends.com/2013/12/09/violations-of-the-constitution-
the-seventh-amendment/

216 http://www.rollingstone.com/politics/news/cruel-and-unusual-punishment
-the-shame-of-three-strikes-laws-20130327

217 http://www.pewresearch.org/fact-tank/2014/04/02/feds-may-be-rethink-
ing-the-drug-war-but-states-have-been-leading-the-way/

218 https://www.themarshallproject.org/2017/09/11/is-there-a-constitutional-
right-to-cash-in-on-the-poor#.UjuYFq1XN

219 https://www.aclu.org/know-your-rights

220 http://constitutionus.com/

221 http://www.census.gov/programs-surveys/acs/methodology/questionnaire
-archive.html

222 http://www.theatlantic.com/politics/archive/2015/06/republicans-try-to-
rein-in-the-census-bureau/395210/

223 http://www.politifact.com/texas/statements/2014/jan/09/us-census-bureau
/americans-must-answer-us-census-bureau-survey-law-/

224 https://www.youtube.com/watch?v=jgsdQxTv5kY

225 http://www.marketingresearch.org/article/major-business-groups-urge-
preservation-census-bureau percentE2 percent80 percent99s-american-
community-survey-acs

226 http://www.opensecrets.org/lobby/index.php

227 http://www.opensecrets.org/lobby/top.php?showYear=2015&indexType=i

228 https://www.americanprogress.org/issues/economy/report/2014/05/02
/88917/how-campaign-contributions-and-lobbying-can-lead-to-inefficient
-economic-policy/

229 http://www.dailykos.com/story/2015/01/12/1357141/—Steven-Brill-60-Minutes
-shows-why-letting-lobbyists-write-the-ACA-was-an-Enormous-Blunder

230 http://www.cfinst.org/data/historicalStats.aspx

231 http://www.rollingstone.com/politics/news/eric-holder-wall-street-double-agent-comes-in-from-the-cold-20150708

232 http://www.huffingtonpost.com/2015/01/15/big-business-lobbying_n_6476600.html

233 http://www.theguardian.com/politics/2014/mar/12/lobbying-10-ways-corprations-influence-government

234 https://www.youtube.com/watch?v=-bYAQ-ZZtEU

235 http://www.cnbc.com/2014/03/28/why-this-84000-drug-costs-just-900-abroad.html

236 http://www.fns.usda.gov/sites/default/files/pd/SNAPsummary.pdf

237 http://dailycaller.com/2014/06/30/11-things-you-didnt-know-you-could-buy-with-food-stamps/

238 http://business.time.com/2013/11/01/5-surprising-things-you-can-buy-with-food-stamps/

239 http://www.fastcompany.com/47593/wal-mart-you-dont-know

240 http://www.nydailynews.com/new-york/brooklyn/study-proves-walmart-super-stores-kill-local-small-businesses-article-1.140129

241 http://www.perkinsgroup.com/industry-trends/big-u-s-firms-shift-hiring-abroad/

242 http://nypost.com/2013/10/05/ibm-now-employs-more-workers-in-india-than-us/

243 http://cis.org/reasoner/migration-equation-big-businessbig-agriculture-big-laborbig-religionbig-immigration

244 http://cis.org/node/1582

245 http://drum.lib.umd.edu/bitstream/handle/1903/8094/umi-umd-5259.pdf?sequence=1&isAllowed=y

246 http://www.nytimes.com/2015/06/04/us/last-task-after-layoff-at-disney-train-foreign-replacements.html

247 http://abcnews.go.com/International/460-million-chinese-residents-suffering-airpocalypse/story?id=44329107

248 https://www.nytimes.com/2015/08/14/world/asia/study-links-polluted-air-in-china-to-1-6-million-deaths-a-year.html

249 http://www.cfr.org/china/chinas-environmental-crisis/p12608

250 Ibid.

251 http://www.cnbc.com/2016/02/11/pollution-crisis-is-choking-the-chinese-economy.html

252 http://www.scmp.com/news/china/article/1409983/rich-nations-outsourcing-pollution-china-says-un-report

253 http://www.reuters.com/article/us-chinapollution-greenpeace-idUS-
    TRE76C5I420110713

254 https://www.washingtonpost.com/graphics/business/batteries/graphite-
    mining-pollution-in-china/

255 https://en.wikipedia.org/wiki/History_of_USDA_nutrition_guides

256 http://www.todayifoundout.com/index.php/2013/09/invented-food-
    pyramid/

257 http://www.whale.to/a/light.html

258 http://time.com/4130043/lobbying-politics-dietary-guidelines/

259 https://www.cdc.gov/NCHS/data/hestat/obesity_adult_07_08/obesity
    _adult_07_08.pdf

260 http://ajph.aphapublications.org/doi/full/10.2105/AJPH.2015.302997

261 http://www.npr.org/sections/health-shots/2016/05/03/476636183/death-
    certificates-undercount-toll-of-medical-errors

262 http://www.theatlantic.com/health/archive/2013/01/new-health-rankings-
    of-17-nations-us-is-dead-last/267045/

263 http://www.cnbc.com/id/100840148

264 http://transform.childbirthconnection.org/wp-content/uploads/2013/01
    /Cost-of-Having-a-Baby1.pdf

265 http://jamanetwork.com/journals/jama/fullarticle/2467552?resultClick=1

266 http://www.aging.senate.gov/imo/media/doc/Drug percent20Pricing per-
    cent20Report.pdf

267 http://abcnews.go.com/Health/generic-prescription-drug-prices-surging-
    families-feeling-squeeze/story?id=31374562

268 https://meps.ahrq.gov/mepsweb/survey_comp/Insurance.jsp

269 https://www.cms.gov/research-statistics-data-and-systems/statistics-
    trends-and-reports/nationalhealthexpenddata/nhe-fact-sheet.html

270 http://surgerycenterok.com/about/

271 http://www.foxbusiness.com/features/2013/06/27/outrageous-er-hospital-
    charges-what-to-do.html

272 https://www.rt.com/usa/266083-hospitals-overcharge-uninsured-cost/

273 http://www.uta.edu/faculty/story/2311/Misc/2013,2,26,MedicalCostsDema
    ndAndGreed.pdf

274 http://object.cato.org/sites/cato.org/files/pubs/pdf/pa-621.pdf

275 http://www.ncpa.org/pub/st296

276 http://scholarship.law.duke.edu/cgi/viewcontent.cgi?article=2905&context
    =faculty_scholarship&sei-redir=1

277 http://www.economist.com/news/finance-and-economics/21604575-drug-companies-are-adept-extending-lifespan-patents-consumers

278 https://www.cms.gov/research-statistics-data-and-systems/statistics-trends-and-reports/nationalhealthexpenddata/nhe-fact-sheet.html

279 Ibid.

280 https://www.census.gov/prod/2002pubs/censr-4.pdf page 59
     https://www.census.gov/prod/cen2010/briefs/c2010br-03.pdf
     https://www.census.gov/population/projections/data/national/2014/summary
     tables.html

281 http://www.jpands.org/vol18no1/foy.pdf

282 http://www.frugaldad.com/media-consolidation-infographic/

283 http://www.forbes.com/sites/vannale/2015/05/22/the-worlds-largest-media-companies-of-2015/#732afc4f2b64

284 https://rsf.org/en/united-states

285 http://www.gallup.com/poll/195542/americans-trust-mass-media-sinks-new-low.aspx?g_source=americans percent27 percent20trust percent20in percent20media&g_medium=search&g_campaign=tiles

286 http://www.journalism.org/2016/06/15/newspapers-fact-sheet/

287 http://ajrarchive.org/article.asp?id=4985

288 http://money.cnn.com/2016/06/15/media/abc-news-disney-orlando-coverage/index.html

289 https://www.truthdig.com/articles/elites-no-credibility-left-interview-journalist-chris-hedges/

290 http://www.cdc.gov/nchs/fastats/leading-causes-of-death.htm

291 http://www.state.gov/j/ct/rls/crt/2014/239418.htm

292 http://www.nyclu.org/pdfs/eroding_liberty.pdf

293 https://edwardsnowden.com/revelations/

294 http://www.gallup.com/poll/195542/americans-trust-mass-media-sinks-new-low.aspx?g_source=americans percent27 percent20trust percent20in percent20media&g_medium=search&g_campaign=tiles

295 http://news.indiana.edu/releases/iu/2014/05/2013-american-journalist-key-findings.pdf

296 http://dailycaller.com/2010/08/28/obama-democrats-got-88-percent-of-2008-contributions-by-tv-network-execs-writers-reporters/

297 https://mediadecoder.blogs.nytimes.com/2012/08/22/donations-by-media-companies-tilt-heavily-to-obama/

298 https://www.publicintegrity.org/2016/10/17/20330/journalists-shower-hillary-clinton-campaign-cash

299 http://www.realclearpolitics.com/articles/2010/02/11/krugman_bushs_deficit_bad_obamas_deficit_good_100258.html

300 http://www.zerohedge.com/news/2017-01-10/paul-krugman-flip-flops-again

301 http://thehill.com/blogs/pundits-blog/media/301285-media-and-trump-bias-not-even-trying-to-hide-it-anymore

302 http://www.nationalreview.com/corner/290292/media-ignores-facts-illegal-immigration-lamar-smith

303 http://www.zerohedge.com/news/2017-01-17/new-abc-wapo-poll-shows-drop-trump-favorabilty-through-aggressive-oversamples

304 http://thehill.com/blogs/pundits-blog/media/301285-media-and-trump-bias-not-even-trying-to-hide-it-anymore

305 http://www.consumerreports.org/cro/magazine/2014/03/too-many-product-choices-in-supermarkets/index.htm

306 http://business.time.com/2011/02/23/why-buying-toothpaste-is-nearly-as-painful-as-a-trip-to-the-dentist/

307 http://www.webmd.com/food-recipes/news/20090323/7-rules-for-eating#1

308 https://www.ag.ndsu.edu/energy/biofuels/energy-briefs/history-of-ethanol-production-and-policy

309 http://www.ncpa.org/pub/ba591

310 http://www.consumerreports.org/cro/news/2013/03/gas-with-ethanol-can-make-small-engines-fail/index.htm

311 http://www.consumerreports.org/cro/news/2011/07/warranties-void-on-cars-burning-e15-say-automakers/index.htmv

312 http://www.ncpa.org/pub/ba591

313 http://www.forbes.com/sites/jamesconca/2014/04/20/its-final-corn-ethanol-is-of-no-use/#26396102ca26

314 http://www.usnews.com/news/articles/2016-02-03/corn-ethanol-the-rise-and-fall-of-a-political-force

315 https://www.downsizinggovernment.org/federal-worker-pay

316 http://www.cnsnews.com/news/article/penny-starr/11588500-words-obamacare-regs-30x-long-law

317 http://www.washingtonexaminer.com/obamacares-2700-pages-are-too-much-for-justices/article/1204606

318 https://fas.org/sgp/crs/natsec/RL31133.pdf

319 http://scholarship.law.ufl.edu/cgi/viewcontent.cgi?article=1686&context=facultypub

320 http://www.nydailynews.com/news/politics/trump-adds-goldman-sachs-executive-administration-article-1.2944943

321 http://billmoyers.com/2013/09/17/hundreds-of-wall-street-execs-went-to-prison-during-the-last-fraud-fueled-bank-crisis/

322 Ibid.

323 http://money.cnn.com/2016/04/28/news/companies/bankers-prison/

324 https://fred.stlouisfed.org/series/TCMDO

325 http://www.pewresearch.org/fact-tank/2014/10/09/for-most-workers-real-wages-have-barely-budged-for-decades/

326 https://journalistsresource.org/studies/economics/inequality/income-inequality-research-distribution-class

327 http://www.gallup.com/poll/192581/americans-confidence-institutions-stays-low.aspx

328 http://www.slate.com/articles/business/it_seems_to_me/1997/05/herb_steins_unfamiliar_quotations.html

329 http://fortune.com/2015/12/10/oil-zombies-debt/

330 http://www.zerohedge.com/news/2016-01-16/exclusive-dallas-fed-quietly-suspends-energy-mark-market-tells-banks-not-force-shale

331 Collins, J. C. (2001). *Good to Great: Why Some Companies Make the Leap . . . and Others Don't*. New York, NY: HarperBusiness.

332 https://herb.ashp.cuny.edu/items/show/1510